How Can They Love The Fruit?

By Willie Muhammad

Table of Contents

Foreword

In this extraordinary book, Student Minister Willie Muhammad shares the impact of the Most Honorable Elijah Muhammad on world affairs. Whereas most scholars have attempted to write the Most Honorable Elijah Muhammad out of history, this book clearly delineates his influence across various spheres of life. Muhammad Ali, in an interview in the *Black Scholar* (1970), noted that the students of Elijah Muhammad were getting all the credit for their accomplishments, but these accolades were misplaced because it was Elijah Muhammad who had rescued them from the bowels of ignorance and stood them up to be warriors for equal justice.

The Most Honorable Elijah Muhammad devoted over 40 years of his life to the liberation of Blacks in America. His life story, from a sharecropper's son to becoming the leader of the Nation of Islam, is remarkable. Born in the area of Sandersville, Georgia, sometime in October of 1897, he witnessed firsthand the brutality of white racial violence. After having a dispute with his employer, he decided to move his family to Hamtramck, Michigan. In April of 1923, he had seen enough of the white racial violence inflicted on Black people to last him 26,000 years (Clegg, 1997; Halasa, 1990; E. Muhammad, 1965).

The search for a better life led him to a destiny that was foretold thousands of years before his birth. While in Detroit, Michigan, he witnessed the killing of Black people. Regarding these experiences, he said in the South they lynch Blacks on trees, but in the North, they shoot them in the streets (E. Muhammad, 1973).

Troubled by the fading hopes and dreams of a better life in the North, Elijah began to find solace in the liquor bottle. His wife, Clara, would have to bring him home after he fell drunk in the alley. His father, perhaps concerned with his son's status, introduced him to a friend named

Abdul (Sahib, 1951). He told Elijah that Abdul was saying some interesting things that could uplift Black people. Initially, Elijah was not too interested because he saw Islam in a negative light (J. Muhammad, 1996). Despite his negative view of Islam, he was intrigued by what he heard from Abdul.

After several attempts to listen to a lecture given by Wallace D. Fard on September 22, 1931, Elijah was able to hear Mr. Fard close up. Wallace D. Fard is the founder of the Nation of Islam who was born in the Holy City of Mecca, Arabia, on February 26, 1877. While listening to Mr. Fard, Elijah reflected on his knowledge of the scripture. His study of the

Bible began as a child, when he poured over scripture and listened to his father's sermons (E. Muhammad, 2006).

After Fard's lecture, it was custom for the listeners to shake his hand. When Elijah came to shake Fard's hand, he whispered into his ear that Fard was the person the Bible described as the second coming of Christ. Fard affirmed Elijah's hunch and told him not to tell anyone (Hakim, 1997). The meeting was so powerful that when Elijah returned home, he told his wife, Clara, to dump all the pork in the trash. While he gave up pork and liquor, the cigarette proved harder to give up (Allah, n.d.).

For the next 3 years and 4 months, Fard and Elijah were inseparable (E. Muhammad, 1974). They spent countless hours together, with Fard teaching Elijah something about everything in the universe (J. Muhammad, 1996). Through narrative pedagogy, Elijah Poole drank from a spiritual cup that caused him to experience a metamorphosis to become Elijah Muhammad (Pitre, 2022).

While the name "Fard" or "Prophet Fard" was used to describe his teacher, Elijah would later refer to him as Master Fard Muhammad. And after Fard's departure, Elijah began to disclose his true identity. Whereas the early followers believed their teacher was a prophet, it was Elijah Muhammad who declared that Allah (God) had appeared in the person of Master Fard Muhammad.

When Fard departed in 1934, he told Elijah Muhammad that he was giving him the hardest job ever given to any person. Elijah's mission was to raise the mentally dead Blacks in America into a spiritual consciousness that would cause them to grow into a new being (E. Muhammad, 1965).

The core of Elijah Muhammad's work was the reeducation of Blacks in America. He said his mission was to raise Blacks from a mentally dead state to one where their creative mind would be birthed (E. Muhammad, 1965, 1974).

The creative mind would give birth to a new world.

As a result of his teachings, Elijah Muhammad became the target of the most powerful people and organizations because the knowledge he shared signaled the end of white rule. Today, the knowledge he brought is fueling modern advances in science and technology, along with other new and emerging fields of study (Pitre, 2021).

Those in power have skillfully kept the Most Honorable Elijah Muhammad out of educational discourse (Pitre, 2015). Moreover, the masses of people do not know the miracle of

Elijah Muhammad and his position in world affairs in the 21st century.

As a testament to his identity, Elijah Muhammad produced a nation of leaders. Those who put his teachings into practice grow into an intellectual and spiritual consciousness that catapults them into leadership. This is best seen in his students, such as Malcolm X, Muhammad Ali, Imam Warith D. Mohammed, Mother Tynnetta Muhammad, and Minister Louis Farrakhan (Pitre, 2022). These students have shaken up the world through a body of knowledge they received from this master teacher, Elijah Muhammad.

In this extraordinary book, Student Minister Willie Muhammad provides jewels of knowledge that demonstrate the impact of Elijah Muhammad's teachings on our modern world. The book is filled with information that, if carefully studied, will serve as a guide to seeing the true identity of Elijah Muhammad.

The book is reader-friendly and provides an authentic narrative that allows readers to ascertain a purity of knowledge that is not diluted by scholarly jargon that misinterprets the teachings of the Most Honorable Elijah Muhammad.

Minister Willie Muhammad's book is an essential work that will add to Elijah

Muhammad studies. Moreover, his book will help readers become a step closer to seeing *Brother Elijah* in his exalted state!

References

Allah, W. (n.d.). *The history of the Nation of Islam: The pioneer years (1930–1950)*. A-Team Publishing.

Black Scholar. (1970, June). "Muhammad Ali," 14–21.

Clegg, C. (1997). *An original man: The life and times of Elijah Muhammad*. St. Martin's Press.

Hakim, N. (1997). *The black stone: The true history of Elijah Muhammad: Messenger of Allah.* M.E.M.P.S. Publications.

Halasa, M. (1990). *Elijah Muhammad: Religious leader.* Chelsea House Publishers.

Muhammad, E. (1965). *Message to the Black man in America.* Final Call.

Muhammad, E. (1973). *The fall of America.* Final Call.

Muhammad, E. (1974). *Our savior has arrived.* Final Call.

Muhammad, E. (2006). *The theology of time.* Secretarius M.E.M.P.S. Publications.

Muhammad, J. (1996). *This is the one: The most honored Elijah Muhammad, we need not look for another* (3rd ed.). Book Company.

Pitre, A. (2015). *The educational philosophy of Elijah Muhammad: Education for a new world.* Hamilton Books.

Pitre, A. (2021). *An introduction to Elijah Muhammad studies* (rev. ed.). Hamilton Books.

Pitre, A. (2022). *Liberation pedagogy—Elijah Muhammad and the art of soul crafting.* Rowman and Littlefield.

Sahib, H. (1951). The Nation of Islam. *Contributions in Black Studies, 13*(1), article 3. https://scholarworks.umass.edu/cibs/vol13/iss1/3

Abul Pitre

Tracy, CA

08/23/2022

CHAPTER 1
Why This Book Has Been Written

Once, while scanning through social media, I came across something that really disturbed me. It was an informational meme that had the following caption: "You know, it's Black

TEACH YOUR KIDS ABOUT

Marcus Garvey
Malcolm X
Assata shakur
Patrice Lumumba
Dr. Frances Cress Welsing
Nat Turner
Harriet Tubman
Huey P Newton
Thomas Sankara
Toussaint louverture
Fred Hampton
khalid Muhammad
Muhammad Ali

History Month. Teach your kids about these."

And when I saw that, it disturbed me, honestly. And the reason why it bothered me was because of what I felt and believe is a GREAT OMISSION! How is it that you can have at least one, two, three students directly impacted by the Teachings of the Most Honorable Elijah Muhammad, and do not even mention the Honorable Elijah Muhammad? In addition to this, they did not even mention the Most Honorable Elijah Muhammad's chief student, the Honorable Minister Louis Farrakhan, who has been and is doing much of what those listed in the graphic wanted to do.

This bothered me because this is a constant theme within the Black community where we want to mention all of these other people, who in truth, brothers and sisters, did not accomplish as much as the Most Honorable Elijah Muhammad accomplished. I do not make such a statement to disrespect them nor to diminish any of their accomplishments. I make that statement from the viewpoint of a historian. Yet, they want to write the Most Honorable Elijah Muhammad out of history?

Those of us who love the Most Honorable Elijah Muhammad cannot keep quiet! If we are quiet, they will write him out of history, and we will be unknowing participants in such a great tragedy. That social media meme first inspired a lecture delivered in our city, New Orleans, and has now formed into this book.

The social media meme is not something new. This effort to leave out the Most Honorable Elijah Muhammad has been afoot for decades, and Allah foretold about such efforts and the failure of these plots in the Holy Qur'an.

"In the name of Allah, the Beneficent, the Merciful. [1](By) the inkstand and the pen and that which they write! [2]By the grace of thy Lord thou art not mad. [3]And surely thine is a reward never to be cut off. [4]And surely thou hast sublime morals. [5]So thou wilt see, and they (too) will see, [6] Which of you is mad. [7]Surely thy Lord knows best who is erring from His way, and He knows best those who go aright." *(Surah 68, verses 1-7)*

"[8]They desire to put out the light of Allah with their mouths, but Allah will perfect His light, though the disbelievers may be averse." *(Surah 61, verse 8)*

In an article titled, "A True Friend: The Honorable Elijah Muhammad," which appeared in The Final Call newspaper, the Honorable Minister Louis pointed out this wicked plan. The Minister said the following:

"In an edition of Ebony magazine, under the byline of Lerone Bennett, 17 historians had gotten together and picked the 50 most important figures in Black American history, and the persons who chose these names are considered by Ebony magazine, 'experts.' Yet, the Honorable Elijah Muhammad was not mentioned. Why? The Honorable Elijah Muhammad's student Malcolm X was mentioned. Would there have been a Malcolm X if there were no Honorable Elijah Muhammad?

The Honorable Elijah Muhammad influenced the writings of James Baldwin, Amiri Baraka, Maya Angelou, John Killens, Louis Lomax and most of the writers who were popular in the 1960s.

His influence is seen today in the writings of Toni Morrison and Alex Haley. His teachings inspired Alex Haley to do the research that led to the book 'Roots.' He influenced playwrights, poets musicians. There is no field of human endeavor among Black people that Elijah Muhammad did not have some positive effect upon.

And now, there is a conscious effort to write the Honorable Elijah Muhammad out of history. However, I am sure that, by the help of God, everyone who plans to write him out of history has already assigned to themselves that chastisement."

These experts mentioned the students of the Most Honorable Elijah Muhammad but did not mention him, a man who had one of the first Black publications that paved the way for Ebony. This is one reason why this book is important. If these experts think that they are doing our people a service by teaching them about all of the other Black leaders and don't see the need to include the historical contributions under the Most Honorable Elijah Muhammad's name, they are unknowingly or knowingly helping to participate in the attempt to write the Most Honorable Elijah Muhammad out of history.

Once again, I am not saying these Black leaders should not be highlighted. We should celebrate them because all of them have given their lives to help in the advancement of Black people in America and around the world. But to teach our children about them and omit the Honorable Elijah Muhammad is doing great harm, because several of the people who are on that list are actually direct— and even indirect—products of the Teachings of the Most Honorable Elijah Muhammad. The impact of the Most Honorable Elijah Muhammad cannot be ignored nor overlooked.

The Honorable Minister Louis Farrakhan continues by saying the following in The Final Call newspaper article:

"The Honorable Elijah Muhammad is indeed a true friend of the Black man and woman because his message is as relevant today as it was when he was physically among us. He worked, suffered, studied and constantly prayed for our rise. He sacrificed his own personal life to devote 44 years to the rise of our people.

He single-handedly, with tenaciousness of will and singleness of purpose, turned the language of America from the use of the word 'Negro,' which means something dead, lifeless or hard, into seeing ourselves as Black people, members of the aboriginal nation of the Earth.

He turned our hearts toward Africa and our brothers and sisters in the isles of the Pacific, Central and South America and the Caribbean.

His Wisdom showed us the connection between the Native Americans and their membership in the aboriginal nation of the Earth. He, more than any religious leader, is responsible for causing us to refer to one another as brothers and sisters.

He caused new levels of scholarship in the research of the history of the Black man; and into the nature and birth record of the Caucasian.

He inspired research into melanin and its presence or absence and its effect on the thought process.

He taught us how to eat to live, causing us to throw away medicines. His teachings on this subject began the process of the beautification of our people, no matter how ugly we appeared to be.

He started the process of reformation of the Black woman, without which there can be no new people.

He showed us the value of a proper education and established a school system that reflected the same. He demonstrated the proper use of money by establishing for his followers, farmland, banks, business, airplanes and airport facilities, international trade and commerce.

You name it, he did it. What a friend we have in Jesus! (The Honorable Elijah Muhammad).

There is not a Black leader who has not been positively affected by this man and his Message.

Without his boldness, would Rev. Jackson dare to speak as he does and run for president? Without his forthrightness in confronting this government for her evil done to Black people, would any of us have the courage to do the same today?

Would you not admit he laid the foundation and opened up the way? What more could a man who loves you do?

But what has been your response to such a friend? The response of many who knew him has been to use his knowledge, but to deny him, to advance self because of him, but never give him any credit.

...

There would be no Louis Farrakhan if there were no Elijah Muhammad; there would be no

Muhammad Ali if there were no Elijah Muhammad. The money that Sugar Ray Leonard, Eddie Murphy, Bill Cosby and others are making today is due to the presence of a new reality in America: the Teachings of the Honorable Elijah Muhammad.

It is sad that so many former followers of the Honorable Elijah Muhammad have helped, knowingly or unknowingly, to write this man out of history."

Questions can be raised about these experts' historical knowledge on Black leadership in America and the world when they fail to include the Most Honorable Elijah Muhammad. Lists of historical figures and others like it would certainly be considered limited without his presence. How much of an NBA expert would you consider someone to be if they left the name of Michael Jordan off their list of "Influential NBA Players?" How much of an expert on Hip-Hop would you consider someone who did not mention Rakim Allah or Jay-Z? I think you get the picture I am painting.

Ask yourself these questions. Where are the students of those on these lists today? Where are their organizations today? We love Brother Marcus Garvey, but where is his organization today? Where are his students? Where are his followers today? The same is unfortunately true with Malcolm X and Patrice Lumumba. Where are their students and followers today? Many of their movements died when they died.

The same enemy that worked day and night to prevent the continued work of those mentioned tried to do it with the Most Honorable Elijah Muhammad and was UNSUCCESSFUL! The same government that went after Huey P. Newton, that went after Fred Hampton, that went after Malcolm X, Marcus Garvey, and Assata Shakur, used all of their power to destroy the legacy of the Most Honorable Elijah Muhammad and the Nation of Islam. Yet, his work remains!

So, shouldn't others be made aware of this miracle? Shouldn't a man whose organization was able to survive, even when he was no longer physically present, be studied? We close this chapter boldly stating, "Yes, he should!"

The reason the enemy was unsuccessful and will continue to be unsuccessful is because the Most Honorable Elijah Muhammad is more than just a Black leader! His leadership is of a divine origin and is backed by the Divine Power. His success over his and OUR enemies is foretold in the scriptures. The Most Honorable Elijah has written many statements speaking about how he and WE would be victorious over his and OUR enemies. Here is one quote from the chapter in the historic book "Message to the Blackman," section titled, "Misunderstanding and Misinterpretation."

"All Messengers were attacked by disbelievers and governments of their time, according to the Qur'an. As an example of what the last Messenger and his followers would face, Pharaoh openly confessed that he desired to slay Moses and did not believe that God (Allah) would be able to protect Moses from his evil plans.

But the Holy Qur'an says that Allah made him an example, for in the last days both Moses and the symbolic lamb are declared to be victorious.

Revelations states that the lamb and his followers, after escaping the evil plans of the beast, sang the song of Moses, which was of the victory over Pharaoh."

As stated by the Most Honorable Elijah Muhammad, the victory is foretold of in the scripture, as shown in the Book of Revelations 15:1-4.

15 Then I saw in heaven another marvelous event of great significance. Seven angels were holding the seven last plagues, which would bring God's wrath to completion. [2] I saw before me what seemed to be a glass sea mixed with fire. And on it stood all the people who had been victorious over the beast and his statue and the number representing his name. They were all holding harps that God had given them. [3] And they were singing the song of Moses, the servant of God, and the song of the Lamb:

Great and marvelous are your works, O Lord God, the Almighty. Just and true are your ways, O King of the nations. [4] Who will not fear you, Lord, and glorify your name? For you alone are holy. All nations will come and worship before you, for your righteous deeds have been revealed."

CHAPTER 2
The Power to Transform Satan

In Chapter 10 of Malcolm X's autobiography, titled, "Satan," he stated the following:

"The prison psychologist interviewed me, and he got called every filthy name I could think of, and the prison chaplain got called worse. My first letter, I remember, was from my religious brother Philbert in Detroit, telling me his 'holiness' church was going to pray for me. I scrawled him a reply I'm ashamed to think of today...I served a total of seven years in prison. Now, when I try to separate that first year—plus that I spent at Charlestown, it runs all together in a memory of nutmeg and the other semi-drugs, of cursing guards, throwing things out of my cell, balking in the lines, dropping my tray in the dining hall, refusing to answer my number—claiming I forgot it—and things like that.

I preferred the solitary that this behavior brought me. I would pace for hours like a caged leopard, viciously cursing aloud to myself. And my favorite targets were the Bible and God. But there was a legal limit to how much time one could be kept in solitary. Eventually, the men in the cellblock had a name for me: 'Satan.' Because of my antireligious attitude."

Pause for a moment and reflect on what you just read. In a prison filled with 'criminals,' Malcolm X's behavior caused other inmates to give him the nickname, "Satan." I point this out to show where Malcolm X was prior to being touched by the Teachings of the Most Honorable Elijah Muhammad.

There are many who try to minimize the Most Honorable Elijah Muhammad's significant role and impact on the life transformation of Malcolm X that made him the man that is so loved. Some scholars have even tried to do the same. They point out how much of an avid reader Malcolm had become while in prison, which he definitely was. However, what cannot be denied is that Malcolm's copying down words in the dictionary and the books he read was not the catalyst for Malcolm Little becoming Malcolm X. If the dictionary and those books were the reason, prisons then and now would be filled with inmates like him. It was the Teachings of the Most

Honorable Elijah Muhammad and Malcolm's correspondence with the Most Honorable Elijah Muhammad that made him who he came to be. This point was highlighted by one of the Nation of Islam's scholars, Dr. Wesley Muhammad, some years ago at an annual panel about Malcolm X, organized by Dr. Marc Lamont Hill. Dr. Wesley stated the following:

"In order to attach to the Malcolm that we want, we have to go all the way before his 13 to 17 years with the Nation of Islam to queer him, because we can't queer Malcolm X or we pigeonhole him to the 350 days when his thought was in flux. Everything to avoid acknowledging a critical fact. Not simply that, Malcolm X that we love is the Malcolm X produced in the womb of the Nation of Islam. Dr. Greg Carr conducted an excellent discussion of the intellectual network that Malcolm Little had available to him before encountering the Most Honorable Elijah Muhammad. He was a well-read man before meeting the Most Honorable Elijah Muhammad, but it was not those intellectual networks that produced the man that the world loves, because a lot of people got knowledge and a lot of people read the books that Malcolm read. What made Malcolm X, Malcolm X, and no longer Malcolm Little or Detroit Red was not the knowledge he acquired from the prison library. But in the Nation of Islam, he got a manhood training that married knowledge to morality and spirituality in a particular way. And the same womb that produced the Malcolm X that we loved, produced the Muhammad Ali, from Cassius Clay we love…"

Dr. Wesley's analysis is spot on. If one reviews Malcolm X's autobiography, we can see that what fully motivated Malcolm X to improve himself educationally was his desire to effectively communicate with the Most Honorable Elijah Muhammad during their written correspondences.

"It was because of my letters that I happened to stumble upon starting to acquire some kind of a homemade education. I became increasingly frustrated at not being able to express what I wanted to convey in letters that I wrote, especially those to Mr. Elijah Muhammad. In the street, I had been the most articulate hustler out there—I had commanded attention when I said something. But now, trying to write simple English, I not only wasn't articulate, I wasn't even functional. How would I sound writing in slang, the way I would say it, something such as 'Look, daddy, let me pull your coat about a cat, Elijah Muhammad—'" *(Chapter 11 of The Autobiography of Malcolm X)*

The Teachings of the Most Honorable Elijah Muhammad woke Malcolm X. His family had converted to

Islam as taught by the Most Honorable Elijah Muhammad, and what they shared during letters and personal visits from the Teachings of the Most Honorable Elijah Muhammad began to raise Malcolm X from the grave of mental death. What Malcolm X learned about the origin and history of the White man and how Blacks had been turned into criminals, and what he read in the library confirmed what he was learning from this little Georgia-born Black man.

> "Mr. Muhammad, to whom I was writing daily, had no idea of what a new world had opened up to me through my efforts to document his teachings in books," stated Malcolm X. *(Chapter 11)*

This added to Malcolm's desire to learn more and more. No matter how many times the significant impact on Malcolm X by the Most Honorable Elijah Muhammad is minimized, the truth cannot be ignored. We would not have Malcolm X if it were not due to Islam as taught by the Most Honorable Elijah Muhammad. A scholar, Malik Mubashir, who served on a panel with Dr. Wesley Muhammad during a symposium, acknowledges the same.

"You know thinking about the Muslim poet Gilardi Rumi when I think of Malcolm. Gilardi Rumi has a parable about an elephant and six blind men. And depending on how they grasp that elephant, they all come away with a different perspective about what the elephant is. For those that grasp the sides, the elephant is like a wall. It's very clear. Some grab the tusks and are like the elephant is a spear. And before long, depending on which part of the elephant they grab, they knew or thought they knew about all that elephant and even came to blows with each because they thought they were all right. Even though they were partially right, but they were all also wrong.

Malcolm X reminds me of that elephant, because depending on what you're looking for in that, depending on what you grab... If you're a Trotskyite, (Malcolm is) getting ready to become a Revolutionary Socialist and join the Socialist Workers Party. If you are a Pan-Africanist with a cultural emphasis, Malcolm's getting ready to join the Pan-African Black Arts Movement. But no matter what side of the elephant you look at, the one that is routinely ignored or used ingenuously, as Dr. Wesley Muhammad said, is the Islamic Malcolm. Without Islam, there is no Malcolm X or el-Hajj Malik Shabazz, and without the Honorable Elijah Muhammad and his word and the womb that that provided for Malcolm's intellectual growth and development, there is, again, no Malcolm X and no el-Hajj Malik Shabazz."

Even Malcolm X in his own words credits the impact of the Most Honorable Elijah Muhammad for making him the man he became.

"The Honorable Elijah Muhammad taught me everything I know and made me everything I am."

In a now released audio recording of Malcolm X reading a letter which he penned himself, he credits the Most Honorable Elijah Muhammad for making him the man he came to be. This letter is regarded as an apology letter to the Most Honorable Elijah Muhammad and can be heard on YouTube. Malcolm states the following:

"I've always known that Master W. D. Fard is Allah. I believe, I believe that Master W. D. Fard is Allah and I believe that you are his Messenger. I believe that your program is right, and I believe that your teachings are right and that it was my belief in this that made me as successful as I was. Especially, it was my firm belief in this that enabled me to stand up in the face of all opposition on television, on radio, before colleges and before people out in the street at mass rallies and support your program and present your program and represent your program. It was my faith in it that enabled me to represent it."

Even when Malcolm left the Nation of Islam and embarked upon establishing his own organization, he still pointed to what he learned from the Most Honorable Elijah Muhammad as the basis of his new direction.

For months, though no longer an active member of the Nation of Islam, Malcolm had not embarked on a public attack of the Most Honorable Elijah Muhammad. After losing the court battle regarding the house that was owned by the Nation of Islam, Malcolm's position turned to a downward spiral. Malcolm was in a pressure cooker by this time. The United States government began to increase its efforts to fracture the relationship between Malcolm and his teacher. As Nation of Islam scholar Brother Demetric Muhammad states, Malcolm's break was manufactured. In his book, "But Didn't You Kill Malcolm? Myth-Busting the Propaganda Against the Nation of Islam," Brother Demetric writes:

> "These were the actions of a man who was an 'organic hypocrite.' These were the actions of a man whose hypocrisy against his teacher and beloved benefactor had been manufactured and cultivated by the enemies of this teacher."

What Brother Demetric states is attested by internal memos exchanged within a COINTELPRO memo. On January 22, 1969, a memo from the special agent in charge of the Chicago FBI office, Marlin Johnson, stated the following:

> "Over the years, considerable thought has been given and action taken with Bureau's approval, relating to methods through which the Nation of Islam, could be discredited in the eyes of the general populace...Or through which factionalism among the leadership could be created...Factionalism disputes have been developed-the most notable being Malcolm X Little."

Malcolm X's contribution while a member of the Nation of Islam and even after his death is appreciated. I am happy that over the last decade, more information is coming out that vindicates the Most Honorable Elijah Muhammad, the Honorable Minister Louis Farrakhan and the Nation of Islam regarding Malcolm's death. Hopefully, more and more people will begin to clearly see the influence of the Most Honorable Elijah Muhammad on many Black leaders, cultural icons and organizations in America and throughout the world.

CHAPTER 3
The Grandfather of the Black Panthers?

The original Black Panther Party was a political organization founded in 1966 by Huey Newton and Bobby Seale to challenge police brutality against the African American community. The Black Panthers organized armed citizen patrols in Oakland and other U.S. cities. At its peak in 1968, the Black Panther Party had 2,000 members. The organization later declined as a result of internal tensions, deadly shootouts and FBI counterintelligence activities aimed at weakening the organization.

Black Panther Party founders Huey Newton and Bobby Seale met in 1961 while students at Merritt College in Oakland, California. They both protested the college's "Pioneer Day" celebration, which honored the pioneers who came to California in the 1800s but omitted the role of African Americans in settling the American West. Seale and Newton formed the Negro History Fact Group, which called on the school to offer classes in Black history.

A simple reading of the history of this organization that worked to better the lives of Black people will reveal that the founders admired the late Malcolm X. In an online article about the Black Panthers, found on Black History in Two Minutes, the following is stated:

> "Electrified by the rhetoric of Malcolm X, founding members Huey P. Newton and Bobby Seale created an organization aimed at protecting the Black community from racism and violence. And thus, the Black Panther Party for Self-Defense was founded in Oakland, Calif., in October of 1966."

This online article makes a point that we intend to delve deeper in, which is the impact of the Most Honorable Elijah Muhammad on the Black Panthers. The Panthers' founders loved and admired Malcolm X, who was a student of the Most Honorable Elijah Muhammad. With that being a well-established fact, we could ask the question, "Is the Most Honorable

Elijah Muhammad like a grandfather to the Black Panthers?"

In two separate interviews, both founders of the Black Panther Party spoke on how Malcolm X impacted them and impacted the founding philosophy of the organization.

In a 1988 interview, Bobby Seal said the following:

> "Huey and I had been involved for some time, off and on, studying Black history, what have you, what Malcolm had done...I was highly influenced by Martin Luther King at first and then later Malcolm X. Largely, the Black Panther Party come out of a lot of readings.... And there we were with all this knowledge about our history, our struggle against racism. And when we started the Black Panther Party, it was more or less based on where Malcolm was coming from, where our struggle was, an argument about the Civil Rights Movement not learning to own property..."

In the Huey P. Newton Reader, Huey said the following:

> "Malcolm X was the first political person in this country that I really identified with...We continue to

believe that the Black Panther Party exists in the spirit of Malcolm . . . the Party is a living testament to his life and work."

Even Eldridge Cleaver, who was another significant figure within the Black Panther Party, talked about how he was influenced by Malcolm X.

One of the hallmarks of the Black Panther Party was its Ten-Point Program. The Ten-Point Program is a set of guidelines for the Black Panther Party and states their ideals and ways of operation, a "combination of the Bill of Rights and the Declaration of Independence."

The document was created in 1966 by the founders of the Black Panther Party, Huey P. Newton and Bobby Seale, whose political thoughts lay within the realm of Marxism and Black Nationalism. Each one of the statements were put in place for all of the Black Panther Party members to live by and actively practice every day. The Ten-Point program was released on May 15, 1967, in the second issue of the party's weekly newspaper, *The Black Panther*. All succeeding 537 issues contained the program, titled, "What We Want Now!"

The Ten-Point Program comprised two sections. The first, titled, "What We Want Now," described what the Black Panther Party wants from the leaders of American Society. The second section, titled, "What We Believe," outlined the philosophical views of the party and the rights that African Americans should have, but are denied. It is structured similarly to the United States Bill of Rights of the U.S. Constitution.

"What We Believe" expands on the first section, making demands of what will be deemed sufficient payment for the injustices committed against the Black community. For example, one section states that, "We believe that this racist government has robbed us and now we are demanding the overdue debt of forty acres and two mules. Forty acres and two mules was promised 100 years ago as a restitution for slave labor and mass murder of black people." It continues, "We will accept this payment in currency which will be distributed to our many communities." Newton and Seale believed that the Black community had been deprived of these benefits over the years, and that the only way to correct this injustice was in repayment of assets that had been lost to them over many years of slavery.

The Ten-Point Program was important for the Black Panther Party because it laid out the "physical needs and all the philosophical principles" they expected and that could be understood by everyone. When Huey Newton talked about the platform, he stated that these things were not something new but something that "black people have been voicing all along for over 100 years since the Emancipation Proclamation and even before that." This platform was essential to the party, because it allowed them to state their wants, needs, and beliefs that people could read and easily understand.

In an interview with Louis Massiah, Huey P. Newton said the following:

> "After we created the, ah, the study classes, I felt that there was a need to do other things, ah, to affect the wider community. And, ah, I became, ah, in contact, I, I came in contact with the Black Muslims. Ah, I was very impressed with Malcolm X. And, ah, Malcolm X's program, or the Honorable Elijah Muhammad, that, ah, Malcolm X followed, program was, ah, ah, it was like a Ten-Point Program. Matter of fact, that, ah, our program was structured after the, ah, patterned after the Black Muslim Program. It, ah, was minus the religion. And, ah, I think that I became disillusioned with the, with the, ah, Muslims after Malcolm X was assassinated. I think that I was following not, ah, Elijah Muhammad or the Muslims but Malcolm X himself."

As you read, Huey Newton admits the Black Panther Party's Ten-Point Program was "structured after" the Nation of Islam's Muslim Program that continues to be printed and displayed on the back cover of EVERY Final Call newspaper and on the official website of the Nation of Islam. The Muslim Program is structured into two sections, "What the Muslims Want" and "What the Muslims Believe." The same was the case for the Black Panther Party's platform, "What We Want" and "What We Believe."

Like many who were unaware of the dirty tricks that J. Edgar Hoover's COINTELPRO was executing against the Nation of Islam, Huey P. Newton had a certain view of the Most Honorable Elijah Muhammad. What if Huey P. Newton would have lived to read the work of Nation of Islam scholars such as Brother Demetric Muhammad and Brother Dr. Wesley Muhammad regarding the role of several United States security and law enforcement agencies working in conjunction to cause a rift within the Nation of Islam and to cause issues between Malcolm X and his Teacher? Would that truth have helped Huey Newton to come out of his "disillusionment" with the Black Muslims and the Most Honorable Elijah

Muhammad? I believe their research, in addition to Huey learning more on how the tactics of COINTELPRO were used against the Panthers, would have changed his mind. Despite how he may have felt, he was undeniably impacted by a student of the Most Honorable Elijah Muhammad, who inspired these young college students and thousands of others based on what the Most Honorable Elijah Muhammad taught him.

We know that the Panthers' founders read and studied the writings, philosophies and works of many. Withstanding that, all of the ideas of those other thought leaders did not impact them the way Malcolm X did. As you read this, ask yourself the following question, "If there was no Malcolm X, would we have had the Black Panthers?" I personally would argue that we would have not. I am not the only who believes this way.

Elijah C. Watson served as Okayplayer's News & Culture Editor. Okayplayer is an online hip-hop and alternative music website and community, described by Rolling Stone as a "tastemaker" and "an antidote to dull promotional Web sites used by most artists." In a review critiquing the documentary titled, "Malcolm X: An overwhelming Influence on the Black Power Movement," Mr. Watson said the following:

> "*Malcolm X* also fails to contextualize X's influence on the Black Power movement. Without X it's arguable that a foundation for the likes of the Black Panther Party, as well as leaders such as Huey Newton, Fred Hampton, Assata Shakur, and Angela Davis wouldn't exist."

Malcolm X was not self-taught. As we discussed, Malcolm was brought from spiritual death to spiritual life by the Most Honorable Elijah Muhammad. The wisdom learned and articulated by Malcolm in hundreds of speeches helped to inspire the Black Panthers.

Years later, the New Black Panther Party was formed. Guess what? It was formed by one, Dr. Khalid Muhammad, who considered himself to be a Believer in the Teachings of who? The Most Honorable Elijah Muhammad.

CHAPTER 4
He was my Saviour

Ali was born on January 17, 1942, in Louisville, Kentucky. His birth name was Cassius Marcellus Clay Jr. At an early age, young Clay showed that he wasn't afraid of any bout—inside or outside of the ring. Growing up in the segregated South, he experienced racial prejudice and discrimination firsthand.

At the age of 12, Clay discovered his talent for boxing through an odd twist of fate. After his bike was stolen, Clay told a police officer, Joe Martin, that he wanted to beat up the thief. "Well, you better learn how to fight before you start challenging people," Martin reportedly told him at the time. In addition to being a police officer, Martin also trained young boxers at a local gym.

Clay started working with Martin to learn how to spar and soon began his boxing career. In his first amateur bout in

1954, he won the fight by split decision. Clay went on to win the 1956 Golden Gloves tournament for novices in the light heavyweight class. Three years later, he won the National Golden Gloves Tournament of Champions, as well as the Amateur Athletic Union's national title for the light heavyweight division.

In 1960, Clay won a spot on the U.S. Olympic boxing team and traveled to Rome, Italy, to compete. At six feet, three inches tall, Clay was an imposing figure in the ring, but he also became known for his lightning speed and fancy footwork. After winning his first three bouts, Clay defeated Zbigniew Pietrzykowski of Poland to win the light heavyweight Olympic gold medal. He won the world heavyweight championship from Sonny Liston in a major upset on February 25, 1964, at age 22.

After all of his accomplishments, Muhammad Ali, though a champion in the sport of boxing, has been referred to by many as not just the Greatest Boxer of All-Time, but the Greatest Athlete! Reflect on that for a moment. When one is labeled as the Greatest Athlete of All-Time, that means he supersedes every athlete in every field of sports, regardless of race and gender. It's no coincidence that the man referred to as the Greatest Athlete of All-Time was another one of the great students of the Most Honorable Elijah Muhammad, who electrified the minds and spirits of Black people and the world!!!

"Few athletes transcend their chosen sport the way Muhammad Ali did. Given his success in the world of boxing, and his actions outside the ring, it can be argued that he is the most important athlete of the 20th century. He gave the sweet science a marketable superstar and used the platform he earned to advance social causes he believed in. There's no shortage of spectacular anecdotes when it comes to Ali. We've compiled 15 stories about the man who called himself 'the greatest of all time' and then did everything possible to live up to that moniker."

(Andrew Champagne, "Muhammad Ali's Secret History That Made Him 'The Greatest'" www.stadiumtalk.com; Jan. 11, 2022)

"What makes a great athlete? How do you define the greatest? Muhammad Ali isn't the best boxer who ever lived. (Boxing guru Bert Sugar ranked him No. 7.) He's not the athlete who brought the most immediate social change. (Jackie Robinson has him there.) And when ESPN released its much-publicized important list of the top 100 athletes of the 20th century, Ali was third, behind Michael Jordan and Babe Ruth.

But there are 23 definitions of the word 'great' in the Oxford English Dictionary. There are more than 135 synonyms. It's a word that can be shaped and shifted into what you want it to be. Through all the meanings and interpretations, one name in sports best encapsulates the abstraction: Muhammad Ali is the greatest athlete in history. Full stop. This is not a knee-jerk reaction of lionizing a man in his passing as our culture is known to do. It's the rightful paean to the most magnetic, charismatic, important, seductive, intelligent, calculating, pioneering, caring, controversial, worldly, self-aware athletic great the world has ever seen. He was so many things to so many people. Whatever you wanted or needed Muhammad Ali to be, he could fill that role. His greatness transcended sport."

(Chris Chase,"Muhammad Ali was the greatest athlete the world will ever see" Fox Sports; June 4, 2016)

"Ali died last week, but his last professional fight was in 1981. Many of us who grew-up in the digital age never actually saw him fight live, but YouTube and ESPN Classic could teach us about his greatness in the ring. However, Ali's reach exceeded the boxing ring. Besides becoming one of the greatest heavyweight boxing champions ever, Ali was great as a person, philanthropist, and entertainer. This explains why many celebrities from all walks of life reacted to his death. Even President Barack Obama said he was the greatest. Nonetheless, Ali does not need any endorsements as his reputation speaks for itself. Here are five reasons Ali was the greatest athlete ever, as well as a great person too."

(Pete D. Camarillo, "Why Ali was the greatest athlete ever" Medium.com; June 12, 2016)

One of the common descriptions about Muhammad Ali is that he transcended his sport. That transcendence began after he accepted Islam and declared his acceptance publicly shortly after becoming a Heavyweight Champion after defeating Sonny Liston. Immediately after professing his faith, this young man not only had to defend himself and his title from many other boxers who wanted to defeat him, but he had to defend his faith and name change from the mainstream public and media. Fueled with the courage the Most Honorable Elijah Muhammad said Islam gives his followers, this young man did just that!

How did Muhammad Ali come to be introduced to Islam? For years this credit was given to Malcolm X, who did help Ali in his growth as a member of the Nation of Islam. However, it was not Brother Malcolm who planted the seeds and helped Muhammad Ali come to Islam. That happened because of TWO OTHER students of the Most Honorable Elijah Muhammad –the Honorable Minister Louis Farrakhan and Brother Abdul Rahman Muhammad.

A Final Call newspaper article titled "Reflections From A Friend And Brother: Minister Abdul Rahman Muhammad On Muhammad Ali" details the relationship between Brother Abdul Rahman Muhammad and Muhammad Ali. Brother Rahman Muhammad first heard the

Teachings of the Most Honorable Elijah Muhammad in 1955, but he did not join the Nation of Islam until 1956, the article says. In March of 1961, Brother Rahman went to Miami, Florida, to assist the Messenger's minister there, Lucius Bey.

"I was selling the newspaper on streets of Miami—at that time it was called Muhammad Speaks. He (Ali–then Cassius Clay) saw me selling the papers and he hollered across the street to me and said, 'Hey brother. Why are we called Negroes? Why are we blind, deaf and dumb? Why is it that everybody else is making progress and we are lacking so far behind?'" said Min. Rahman Muhammad. Those words spoken by the young boxer came from a recording released by then Brother Louis X— Minister Louis Farrakhan—entitled A White Man's Heaven Is A Black Man's Hell. "He was quoting that to me," continued Min. Rahman Muhammad. "So, when he said that, I said, 'hey brother, you're hip to the teachings.' He said, 'yeah, I am Cassius Clay and I'm going to be the next heavyweight champion of the world.' From that day on, he and I were friends and I began to mentor him and teach him. That same day he took me down to his room and showed me his scrapbook and showed me press clippings of Ingemar Johansson. He was the heavyweight champion at that time. He had a rematch with Floyd Patterson. Well, Ali was boxing with Johansson at that time as a sparring partner in Miami, but Ali was beating up on the champ. So they wrote in the paper, 'this brash kid from Louisville, is about to mess up a four million dollar gate because he's beating up on the champ.' I saw and read that and saw how cocky Ali was," Min. Abdul Rahman said chuckling. "I said to myself then, that if I look out for this brother, he probably would be champ. So, from that day on I took him under what some might say, 'my wing.' I showed him what was in the streets, sat with him in hotel lobbies and showed him pimps, boosters, prostitutes and hustlers. I just showed him the way of life that goes on in America amongst Black people. Then I began to teach him the ways and deceitfulness of White people, which we know the Honorable Elijah Muhammad taught us that they are arch-deceivers. So, I conveyed these teachings to Cassius Clay. And I began to lay it on him and he got stronger and stronger in teachings of the Honorable Elijah Muhammad."

Muhammad Ali also clearly expressed the impact that the Most Honorable Elijah Muhammad had on his life. Here are a few quotes provided by Nation of Islam researcher, Brother Demetric Muhammad, in an article titled, "Muhammad Ali's Beloved Teacher, the Most Honorable Elijah Muhammad."

"From Thomas Hauser's book Muhammad Ali: His Life and Times:

"The first time I heard about Elijah Muhammad was at a Golden Gloves Tournament in Chicago [in 1959]. Then, before I went to the Olympics, I looked at a copy of the Nation of Islam's newspaper, Muhammad Speaks. I didn't pay much attention to it, but a lot of things were working on my mind. When I was growing up, a colored boy named Emmett Till was murdered in Mississippi for whistling at a white woman. Emmett Till was the same age as me, and even though they caught the men who did it, nothing happened to them. Things like that went on all the time. And in my own life, there were places I couldn't go, places I couldn't eat. I won a gold medal representing the United States at the Olympic Games, and when I came home to Louisville, I still got treated like a nigger. There were restaurants I couldn't get served in. Some people kept calling me 'boy.' Then in Miami in 1961, I was training for a fight, and met a follower of Elijah Muhammad named Captain Sam [Minister Abdul Rahman Muhammad]. He invited me to a meeting, and after that, my life changed."

"In a November 1975 Playboy magazine interview the champ stated:

"He was my Jesus, and I had love for both the man and what he represented. Like Jesus Christ and all of God's prophets, he represented all good things... Elijah Muhammad was my savior, and everything I have came from him—my thoughts, my efforts to help my people, how I eat, how I talk, my name."

Muhammad Ali went on to discuss how he would like to be remembered:

"I'll tell you how I'd like to be remembered: as a Black man who won the heavyweight title and who was humorous and who treated everyone right. As a man who never looked down on those who looked up to him and who helped as many of his people as he could—financially and also in their fight for freedom, justice and equality. As a man who wouldn't hurt his people's dignity by doing anything that would embarrass them. As a man who tried to unite his people through the faith of Islam that he found when he listened to the Honorable Elijah Muhammad. And if all that's asking too much, then I guess I'd settle for being remembered only as a great boxing champion who became a preacher and a champion of his people. And I wouldn't even mind if folks forgot how pretty I was."

Muhammad Ali went on to impact many other athletes. Just go and research the historic meeting that took place in the city of Cleveland between Muhammad Ali and many other great athletes of that time. The meeting came to be known as the "Cleveland Summit." In his book,

Kareem Abdul Jabbar, known then as Lew Alcindor, wrote about how he was impacted by Muhammad Ali's stance. After the meeting in Cleveland, the basketball great realized he had the responsibility to use his platform, whatever the cost, to speak out against racism and injustice. He wrote in his book "Becoming Kareem: Growing Up On and Off the Court," published years later:

> "Being at the summit and hearing Ali's articulate defense of his moral beliefs and his willingness to suffer for them reinvigorated my own commitment to become even more politically involved."

All of this was inspired by Muhammad Ali's stance regarding America's involvement in the Vietnam War. On April 28, 1967, while staying in Houston, Muhammad Ali was told to report to an Army induction office, according to The Atlantic. The inducting officer called his name repeatedly, but Ali did not step forward, stating:

"My conscience won't let me go shoot my brother, or some darker people, or some poor hungry people in the mud for big powerful America.

And shoot them for what? They never called me n*gger, they never lynched me, they didn't put no dogs on me, they didn't rob me of my nationality, rape and kill my mother and father ... Shoot them for what? How can I shoot them poor people? Just take me to jail."

According to the New York Times, Ali had taken an exam to get drafted into the army at age 18 but scored poorly, meaning he was eligible to be drafted only in times of war or national emergencies. But then-President Lyndon B. Johnson expanded military operations in Vietnam, so the army lowered requirements to be drafted. Ali, who was sure he wasn't going to be drafted, was called up for service. He refused on grounds of religion and was arrested then convicted. He avoided jail time while his case was being tried, but the damage was done.

His comments were not taken lightly. The war was popular at that time, and the public did not appreciate his words. Public figures derided him on national television, with some calling for him to be jailed. Even Jackie Robinson, the first African American to play in Major League Baseball and a former military officer, was critical of Ali, saying his refusal hurt the morale of young African American soldiers in Vietnam.

Ali lost his boxing licenses, was stripped of his titles and was unable to participate in fights for three years. His trainer, Angelo Dundee, told ESPN that this cost him his best, prime fighting years.

"Due to his beliefs, he was robbed of the best years of his life — that's a subject that we must not forget, ever," Dundee said. "Clay was speed, harmony in motion, an extraordinary sight to see. It seemed impossible to hit him. Ali, the guy that came back after his inactivity, was more flat-footed; he had to go in and fight and take more punishment."

In the meantime, Ali visited college campuses, where anti-Vietnam War sentiments were growing. It was not until 1971 that the U.S. Supreme Court overturned Ali's conviction and he was able to regain his boxing license.

Many writers and historians like to explain Muhammad Ali's refusal to participate in the war in general terms, "his religious beliefs." The straight truth is, he refused because of what he learned from the Most Honorable Elijah Muhammad.

Muhammad Ali's first anti-Vietnam War remark, according to his autobiography—"We ain't got nothing against no Viet Cong"—occurred in Miami, in front of a group of children. It was repeated in front of reporters.

In an article printed in The Final Call newspaper, writer Jehron Muhammad speaks about how Muhammad Ali's meeting with the Most Honorable Elijah Muhammad further encouraged him in his stance. Brother Jehron writes:

> "One thing that gave him strength and helped him hold his position was a meeting with Elijah

Muhammad, where he told Ali, 'Brother, if you felt what you said was wrong, then you should be a man and apologize for it. And likewise, if you felt what you said was right, then be a man and stand up for it."

Ali went on to make similar statements, such as:

"Why should they ask me to put on a uniform and go ten thousand miles from home and drop bombs and bullets on brown people in Vietnam while so-called Negro people in Louisville are treated like dogs and denied simple human rights?

No, I am not going ten thousand miles from home to help murder and burn another poor nation simply to continue the domination of white slave masters of the darker people the world over. This is the day when such evils must come to an end. I have been warned that to take such a stand would put my prestige in jeopardy and could cause me to lose millions of dollars which should accrue to me as the champion.

But I have said it once and I will say it again. The real enemy of my people is right here. I will not disgrace my religion, my people or myself by becoming a tool to enslave those who are fighting for their own justice, freedom and equality...

If I thought the war was going to bring freedom and equality to 22 million of my people they wouldn't have to draft me, I'd join tomorrow. But I either

49

have to obey the laws of the land or the laws of Allah. I have nothing to lose by standing up for my beliefs. So I'll go to jail. We've been in jail for four hundred years."

And:

"It is in the light of my consciousness as a Muslim minister and my own personal convictions that I take my stand in rejecting the call to be inducted. ... I find I cannot be true to my beliefs in my religion by accepting such a call. I am dependent upon Allah as the final judge of those actions brought about by my own conscience."

In a 1967 interview, he stated:

"My conscience won't let me go shoot my brother, or some darker people, or some poor hungry people in the mud for big powerful America. And shoot them for what? They never called me nigger, they never lynched me, they didn't put no dogs on me, they didn't rob me of my nationality, rape and kill my mother and father. ... Shoot them for what? How can I shoot them poor people? Just take me to jail."

He said something very similar later when he talked to the journal, The Black Scholar, in 1970:

"I met two black soldiers a while back in an airport. They said: 'Champ, it takes a lot of guts to do what you're doing.' I told them: 'Brothers, you just don't know. If you knew where you were going now, if you knew your chances of coming out with no arm or no eye, fighting those people in their own land, fighting Asian brothers, you got to shoot them, they never lynched you, never called you nigger, never put dogs on you, never shot your leaders. You've got to shoot your 'enemies' (they call them) and as soon as you get home you won't be able to find a job. Going to jail for a few years is nothing compared to that.'"

All one needs to do is to study the Muslim Program of the Nation of Islam to see where Muhammad Ali was given reason not to fight in the wars of America. If one were to read the Muslim Program, he/she would see that not participating in unjust American wars is not a political position of the Nation of Islam, but rather, part of the belief system of its members. It is stated in "What the Muslims Believe":

10. WE BELIEVE that we who declare ourselves to be righteous Muslims, should not participate in wars which take the lives of humans. We do not believe this nation should force us to take part in such wars, for we have nothing to gain from it unless America agrees to give us the necessary territory wherein we may have something to fight for."

Did not Muhammad Ali say the same thing? Yes, he emphatically did! He made these statements because of what he was taught from his teacher. Take a moment and read these words from the Most Honorable Elijah Muhammad on the Vietnam War and what role Blacks should play.

"The fight over in Vietnam is not a fight of yours. It is not a fight of mine. They are not the people that my God sent after, trying to save, Vietnam people, nor the white American's, who are fighting them. We have nothing to do with that and I will tell anyone, regardless to who it is, and regardless to how wise he is, I will tell him, 'You are not wise enough, yet, to tell me to go to Vietnam to fight."

("The Theology of Time" by Messenger Elijah Muhammad; June 18, 1972)

"You didn't need to go over to Vietnam to fight. No! What are you going to fight for? If America wins, you still will be her slave nigger, and she will have Vietnam besides you? You won't win.

("The Theology of Time" by Messenger Elijah Muhammad; July 9, 1972)

In addition to the words of his teacher, Muhammad Ali also had the example of his teacher, who himself refused to fight in World War II. As a result, he was arrested, even though he was past the age requirement. In 1942, the Most Honorable Elijah Muhammad was arrested. In the book "Message to the Blackman in America," in the chapter titled, "Un-American," the Most Honorable Elijah Muhammad talks about his arrest and his reasoning behind his position.

> "The next time I was arrested was May 8, 1942, in Washington, D.C., by the F.B.I. for not registering for the draft. When the call was made for all males between 18 and 44, I refused (NOT EVADING) on the grounds that, first, I was a Muslim and would not take part in war and especially not on the side with the infidels. Second, I was 45 years of age and was NOT according to the law required to register. The above can be verified with the court records in Detroit and Washington D.C."

It's clear where Muhammad Ali received the idea and stance regarding fighting for a country that EVEN during the time of the Vietnam War was depriving Black people of freedom, justice and equality and actively working to destroy and discredit Black leaders and Black organizations.

We opened this chapter talking about how Muhammad Ali is regarded as the greatest, the best and the highest athlete in the world! It's no coincidence that the Most Honorable Elijah Muhammad named him Muhammad Ali. Muhammad means, "one worthy of praise and praised much," and Ali means, "high and elevated." The success that Muhammad Ali accomplished as a boxer and an activist reflects the name given to him by the Most Honorable Elijah Muhammad. This name was given to him early in his practice of Islam as taught by the Most Honorable Elijah Muhammad.

We are just in the beginning of this book, and we have only talked about two of the many giants the Most Honorable Elijah Muhammad produced from the body of knowledge he received from his Teacher, Master Fard Muhammad.

Malcolm and Ali were two of the Most Honorable Elijah Muhammad's students who gained national recognition. He produced many other leaders that were shaking up their respective cities. To continue to try to minimize the impact of this man is a sin of great proportion!

I close this chapter with words from Brother Abdul Rahman Muhammad and by Muhammad Ali himself regarding the impact of the Messenger.

> "'But what appalls me,' said the Nation of Islam pioneer, listening to media reports concerning Muhammad Ali's champ's passing, 'is that the world is giving credit to the pupil and never to the teacher. The Honorable Elijah Muhammad, who was the teacher of Malcom (X), was also the teacher of Warith Deen Muhammad and the teacher of Minister Louis Farrakhan. And of all those men, everybody is made to worship the pupil. But the Minister Louis Farrakhan, he refuses to allow you to worship him because, he keeps the Honorable Elijah Muhammad out front, letting you know where he got his teaching from and where he got his spirit from. So in the case of Muhammad Ali, the world is trying to make you believe that he was courageous and that he did all this on his own. But his character, his morals were built through the teachings of the Honorable Elijah Muhammad.

Muhammad Ali knew that. But the world make you want to believe that he was some freak of nature that jumped up and had enough nerve to buck the whole system called the United States of America,' he said."

Let's not forget what Muhammad Ali said about the Most Honorable Elijah Muhammad's impact on him as well. It is worth repeating.

"He was my Jesus, and I had love for both the man and what he represented. Like Jesus Christ and all of God's prophets, he represented all good things... Elijah Muhammad was my savior, and everything I have came from him—my thoughts, my efforts to help my people, how I eat, how I talk, my name."

CHAPTER 5
Islam and Blacks in America

According to the Pew Research Center, in the early 20th century, Islam had little presence in most parts of the United States. The religion had a foothold in many Black urban communities. At the time of the 2019 article, Black people (not including those of Hispanic descent or mixed race) made up 20% of the United States' overall Muslim population. Two percent (2%) of Black Americans identify as Muslims. Forty-nine percent (49%) are converts to Islam. Compared to other levels of religious conversion, the conversion rate of Blacks to Islam is high.

Any time the rise and spread of Islam in America is discussed, the discussion must include the Most Honorable Elijah Muhammad. If he is not mentioned, the discussion is lacking and does not capture the true historical picture of how Islam took root in America. The way Islam rose is a result of the Most Honorable Elijah Muhammad. The Pew

Research Center article goes on to further say:

> "In the early 1900s, some Muslim religious leaders in the U.S. asserted that Islam was the natural religion of black people, broadly drawing upon the narratives of African Muslims captured centuries ago and sold as slaves in the Americas. Most prominent among the groups saying this was the Nation of Islam, which was originally founded in 1930 and is currently led by Minister Louis Farrakhan. Today, just two of every 100 black Muslims surveyed say they currently identify with the Nation of Islam. Instead, most black Muslims say they are either Sunni Muslims (52%) or identify with no particular Islamic denomination (27%)."

As we have been stating all throughout this book, there is an effort to minimize and/or downright ignore the impact of the Most Honorable Elijah Muhammad on the direction of Black America and even on the spread of Islam in America. In the survey, one critical question was not asked to the participants, which should have been asked. Any person who truly knows the significance of the Most Honorable Elijah Muhammad would know that this question should be asked. The omission of this important question during the survey was admitted to and is stated as follows:

> "However, it is worth noting that the 2017 survey did not ask Muslims if they had
> ever *previously* identified with the Nation of Islam – an important point because many black Muslims, including prominent American Muslim figures such as Muhammad Ali, Malcolm X and Imam W. Deen Mohammed, were members of the Nation of Islam before coming to associate with other types of Islam."

The Nation of Islam under the Most Honorable Elijah Muhammad and his students helped to make Black America more familiar with Islam. This created an atmosphere that caused people to be less hostile to those who practiced Islam. They either joined the Nation of Islam or accepted some other type of Islam as stated in the quote. This impact of the Nation is not given enough credit nor attention. Many of the buildings that are masjids today in Muslim communities that cater to Blacks (primarily Imam Warith Deen Mohammed's community), are buildings that were once temples of the Nation of Islam. Many of the imams were former ministers of the Most Honorable Elijah Muhammad. The Most Honorable Elijah Muhammad even inspired the flag of the late Imam Warith Deen Mohammed's community. The Imam wrote the following when he explained the new flag:

"We have a new creation that is really the creation of the Honorable Master Elijah Muhammad (may the peace of Allah be on him), even though I may be given the credit for putting it together. Some of you, especially the sisters and brothers who were very close to him, will remember the vision that he used to tell us about. He said that he saw a book and its letters were dimensional (they had depth). He also said that when he looked at the letters of the book, it appeared as though the letters were penetrating the book all the way through. These letters had a glow or an illumination. The only letter that he recognized was the Arabic letter 'lam'

The 'lam' in Arabic is the letter 'L.' The Honorable Elijah Muhammad said that he recognized it because that letter seemed to have been all through the book and that it stood out all through the writing. When he told me that I listened very attentively to him as I always did, especially when he seemed to be really concerned about what he was talking about, or engrossed, so to speak, in what he was talking about. As I listened to him very closely, I was trying to interpret the vision that he was telling me about. There were others at the table that day when he talked about his vision. I said to myself, 'What can this 'lam' stand for? What can it represent?' I knew that there was no other book coming to Muslims after the Holy Quran, but the Holy Quran. So, I knew that it could not mean that a physical book was coming after the Holy Quran to replace the Holy Quran. Although he had said things to that effect, I understood him. I knew that he did not actually mean what we thought he was saying — he meant something else. He meant that a great understanding, a new way of looking at the book, was coming. So, in our life, it would be like a new book coming in.

Then, it came to me. I said, 'My father is telling us that the new book that is to come is really a new book to us because we have never known the Holy Quran.' We have known the Bible. Most of us know much more about the Bible than we know about the Holy Quran. In fact, for most of the years of the Honorable Elijah Muhammad's leadership, he did not allow the Holy Quran to be preached or to be handed out freely among the believers, but he always held it up high as 'the book.' He said that the Holy Quran was the pure book, but he never encouraged us to really get into it. I knew that his vision of a new book was a vision of the Holy Quran, but it was vague in my mind. The idea, or the thing that I was seeing, had not taken complete form, so I put it aside.

While I was trying to think of a new drawing for the mosque blackboard, the picture came to form. I said that the vision should not be a drawing for the blackboard, but it should be the new flag for the Lost-Found Nation of Islam.

The new flag is really a book, and the book is the Holy Quran. On the book is written 'La ilaha ill – Allah,' which means, 'There is nothing worthy of worship as a god but Allah,' and 'Muhammad – un Rasulu-llah,' which means that Muhammad is the Messenger of Allah. If you have some knowledge of the contents of the Holy Quran, you know that this first principle (kalimah) or pillar of faith, is all through the Holy Quran from cover to cover. It dominates the whole Holy Quran. If you count the number of times that the letter 'lam' is repeated in that kalimah, you will see that it stands out more than any other letter in the kalimah. When you look at it, you see 'lam' before you see anything else.

So, this was his vision. I think that the Honorable Master Elijah Muhammad (peace be on him) should get the credit for this vision, and I think that it is a flag that you all can identify with and be proud of. A new world needs a new flag. The Muslim world has come to be identified with the symbol of the crescent and the star, but when you read the Holy Quran you do not find any crescent and star in there.

Islam is a simple religion; that is, it is not a religion that is covered up with symbolism or ritualism. It is a religion that comes straight forward and straight out in the open with what it is all about. What brought on the Islamic flags with the emblem of the star and the crescent was the Christian crusades that came against Islam. The leaders of the

Christian army carried the cross, so the Muslims, reacting to that, raised the crescent. The crescent was a better symbol because the cross represents death. So, here was an army representing a nation or society of people that held sacred an emblem of death, and they could not see the ugliness of what they were doing. All they knew was that it was Jesus that they identified with. When you really think about it, the lifting of the cross as something sacred really is a disgrace to the beautiful world that Jesus brought into existence.

The emblem itself brings to mind death and misery — it does not bring to mind life. You have to interpret 'Jesus' to arrive at life as a meaning for the cross. You have to connect Jesus, his purpose, his sacrifice, and his teaching with the emblem—but how many of us will see the cross and do all of that interpreting? When we see it, we see something that is on graveyards. We think of the suffering and the misery that Jesus had to bear. To us, it is an emblem of death and shame and suffering. So, the star and the crescent is a better emblem to us than the cross.

What the Muslims were saying to the Christians is this: 'You lift up death and you see death as glory, but God has pointed out in His scripture that His glory is readily seen — not in the grave, but in the heavens.' Read the Bible from Genesis to Revelation. God never points to the graveyard to show us His glory. He says that we should look at the heavens and how they are lifted up in glory— the sun, the moon, and the stars. Muslims were saying to the Christians that the sign of God's glory is not death, but life, and that the sun is the source of life in this physical world and the moon is a necessity. The stars are very useful to man because they direct his path at sea and through the land.

So, the Muslims raised a much better sign, but they did not raise the sign upon orders from Prophet Muhammad (peace and blessings of Allah be upon him). They raised it as an answer to the cross that was raised in war against them. What should we really exalt? What should we really raise? It is knowledge!

We know that emblems cannot save humanity and pictures and signs cannot save humanity. Men can look at the stars and the moon in the sky all their life, for generation after generation, until the land grows old and dead. That does not mean that they are going to be lifted up as a society. The savage, primitive man and woman see the sun, moon, and stars but what has made the difference? Knowledge.

The book of knowledge for the Muslims is the Holy Quran. If we exalt anything other than knowledge, we exalt the wrong thing. You may ask, 'What about God?' God is not something that we know in any sense other than in a body of knowledge. We do not know God in flesh and we do not know God in symbols. We know God in knowledge. You may say, 'I feel God in my flesh and that is how I know God.' That is only the beginning of knowledge. Feelings are the beginning of knowledge, but you cannot say that you 'know' until you grow up a little bit taller than feelings."

The flag inspired by the Most Honorable Elijah Muhammad still flies over the community his son established was inspired by his father. I mention this to show the impact of the Most Honorable Elijah Muhammad.

I mentioned earlier how very few of these "experts" actually give the Most Honorable Elijah Muhammad the credit he deserves for the spread of Islam in America. However, surprisingly someone who is not a fan of the Most Honorable Elijah Muhammad begrudgingly admitted to the critical role the Most Honorable Elijah Muhammad plays in the spread of Islam in America. This critic, who admitted such, is a writer by the name of Daniel Pipes. He wrote an article titled, "How Elijah Won," in June 2000. Mr. Pipes opens his article by stating the following:

> "In the early 1930's, when the Nation of Islam had just come into existence, its founder made the bold prediction that, one day, Islam would replace Christianity as the primary faith of black Americans. At the time, this assertion must have sounded incredible, if not slightly mad; not only was the Islamic faith broadly despised in the United States,

but African-Americans who were Muslim numbered at that time only in the dozens. By 1959, however, a perverse endorsement of this same prediction would issue from, of all people, a top leader of the Ku Klux Klan. In a letter to the New York City police commissioner, that white supremacist wrote: 'If we fail to stop the Muslims now, the sixteen million niggers of America will soon be Muslims, and you will never be able to stop them.'

Today, that 1930's prediction no longer seems so outlandish - indeed, it has already been partially borne out. About one million African-Americans now identify themselves as Muslims, and a visit to the black sections of any fair-sized American town quickly confirms the presence not only of an Islamic infrastructure - mosques, schools, halal butchers, stores carrying Islamic clothing - but of an active and ambitious drive to propagate Islam. So vital is this movement that the director of a Christian effort to stem its headway has made a memorable prediction of his own: 'If the conversion rate continues unchanged, Islam could become the dominant religion in black urban areas by the year 2020.'

Is there a single figure most responsible for the remarkable career of Islam among African-Americans? Undoubtedly, the most common reply to this question would name the man who was born as Malcolm Little and died as El-Hajj Malik El-Shabazz, and is best known as Malcolm X (1925-65). Charismatic, eloquent, honest, a martyred seeker of true faith, Malcolm X did play a major role in the development of black Islam, and to this day

many American blacks cite his
1964 *Autobiography* as a powerful factor in their
own conversion to the faith. Yet Malcolm X's active
career as a Muslim lasted not much over a decade;
his real contribution lies elsewhere, as an apostle of
secular black nationalism. Today, he is a pop-
culture icon, his memory kept alive by Spike Lee's
movie about him and by baseball caps sporting his
"X," T-shirts emblazoned with his face, and a U.S.
postal stamp in his honor.

In the final analysis, it was another man, Malcolm
X's mentor, who had the greater impact on
establishing Islam among African-Americans. This
was the uncharismatic, inarticulate, heterodox, and
long-lived Elijah Muhammad."

Though the article is an attack piece
on the Most Honorable Elijah Muhammad,
the writer is right. When the history is
written, those who do real scholarship
will have to give credit where credit is
due. Mr. Pipes tries to paint the Most
Honorable Elijah Muhammad as a filthy
and immoral man. He is wrong in his
effort to do so. Daniel Pipes was born
from Jewish parents. From what I have
read of him, his faith is from Judaism. The
Most Honorable Elijah Muhammad's
domestic life is right in line with the
domestic lives of the Prophets of both the

Bible and the Qur'an. The Most Honorable Elijah Muhammad did not impregnate teenage girls, as Malcolm out of anger described minutes after in a court of law. He stated during a trial that the Most Honorable Elijah Muhammad had wives. The Most Honorable Elijah Muhammad reformed thousands of people and made them into a Nation based upon submission to Allah. An immoral man cannot do such. Despite, Mr. Pipes' moral attacks, I am thankful God allowed him to see how Elijah INDEED won!

CHAPTER 6
The Influence of How to Eat to Live on Black America's Dietary Law

While preparing for this chapter, I researched several of the platforms of some of our great leaders who worked to improve the condition of our people here in America. I examined the works of Marcus Garvey and Noble Drew Ali, both of whom are honored and respected by the Nation of Islam. As I searched their platforms, I specifically searched for information that would show any dietary guidance either of these men included in their platform to better our community. Based upon this brief examination, I discovered the closest thing to be found in this regard was that Marcus Garvey of the United Negro Improvement Association organized the Black Cross Nurses, which was started by Lady Henrietta Vinton Davis. On the UNIA governing body website, the following description is posted about the Black Cross Nurses:

The lead up to the Black Cross Nurses is the 1918 Flu Pandemic that Hon. Marcus Garvey realized left Africans medically unprotected and defenseless. As such, the concept of a hands-on medical first aid organization was developed. Lady Henrietta Vinton Davis first learned of the work of the Hon. Marcus Garvey and the UNIA while traveling the Caribbean in 1917 and 1918. She was so impressed with Garveyism that in 1920, at the age of sixty, she gave up her stage career to work full-time for the UNIA. She would become the organization's first international organizer, a director of the Black Star Line, and the second vice-president of the Negro Factories Corporation. She was also one of the signatories of the Declaration of the Rights of the Negro Peoples of the World at the UNIA♦ACL First International Convention in New York City in August 1920. Most importantly, she founded the (Universal) Black Cross Nurses in Philadelphia in 1920.

The Black Cross Nurses served as the women's auxiliary of the UNIA, placing women in a supportive role, while the men's auxiliary – African Legion – served in a protective role. Mr. Garvey wanted everyone in the UNIA to feel they belonged within the organization, and the Black Cross Nurse served that purpose for women. Local chapters were established with a matron head nurse, secretary, and treasurer to provide health services and hygiene education to Black people. Few programs existed which would admit people of African descent into nursing training at the time and many health facilities provided unequal care to Black people; one of the goals of the

Black Cross Nurses was addressing these discrepancies. Black doctors, nurses and lay practitioners took courses ranging from six months to a year to make sure that standardized care was being given. In addition, upon graduation from the course, each member was required to purchase and wear their official uniform. In many ways, the Black Cross Nurses functioned as a social reform movement, while developing role models for young women.

The Black Cross Nurses promoted education, good health and hygiene, juvenile rehabilitation, maternal and infant care, and training in proper nutrition. It also provided a professional, organized structure for members, giving them a means to appear in roles of public leadership. In articles which appeared in the Negro World, Black Cross Nurses addressed a wide variety of topics from advice to expectant mothers to contagious diseases, heart disease, and hygiene, as well as treatment options. Benevolent community service included distributing clothing and food to those in need."

As I researched information on Noble Drew Ali, the closest I could find was the following:

"In 1927, Moorish Science Temple founder Noble Drew Ali created the Moorish Manufacturing Corporation to market his line of healing teas, tonics, and oils."

In effect, I was unable to find a detailed dietary plan or program similar to what the Most Honorable Elijah Muhammad presented in his monumental books titled, "How to Eat to Live." This point is not highlighted to serve as disregard or to discredit the noble and honorable work of these great men. Rather, this point is lifted to bear witness to the comprehensive and now evidence-supported program given to us by the Messenger of Allah.

It is also worth noting that I did come across an online article on www.eater.com, titled, "Homecoming," which was written by Ameriah Mercer on January 14, 2021. The article mentioned that a few Black religious groups encouraged a dietary lifestyle contrary to the dietary habits our ancestors developed to survive. The author stated the following:

> Plant-based eating survived in Black culture in part through religious groups that were focused less on proving their humanity to white people and more on finding fulfillment within, and for, themselves.

These radical communities saw spiritual and intellectual freedom — not necessarily social integration — as critical to success. Like many Black vegan influencers today, their goal was to use food as a tool in paving a way toward higher consciousness.

The Seventh-day Adventists, a Protestant sect that established African-American membership as early as the mid-1800s, have encouraged a vegetarian diet since 1863, when one of its members, believed to be a prophet, articulated a vision they had on the subject. Many Adventists today are vegetarian, and 32 percent of Adventists are Black. The African Hebrew Israelites of Jerusalem, who believe Black Americans are descendants of the ancient Hebrews of the Bible, also promoted vegetarianism in African-American culture. Today, the majority of their estimated 400,000 to 500,000 members in the U.S. consume a strict vegan diet.

Followers of Rastafarianism are probably the best-known for seeking a natural, holistic diet. The religion was birthed in the 1930s in Jamaica and built upon the philosophies of Marcus Garvey, who organized a Black nationalist movement in the U.S. in the 1920s. Many Rastafarians adhere to an 'Ital' diet, which focuses on organic foods from the earth that increase one's connection with nature and God. Since they consider meat to be dead, they believe that eating it works against one's natural energy; while most Rastafari are vegetarian, some are strict vegans."

I was pleased to find that the article specifically highlights the impact of the Most Honorable Elijah Muhammad on the dietary evolution of Black people in America.

"Of all the religious groups, the Nation of Islam were considered the most radical in their promotion of vegetarianism. They were unapologetic in using plant-based eating as a way to challenge racist oppression in America. In 1967 and 1972, Elijah Muhammad, who led the Nation of Islam for four decades, published two volumes of *How to Eat to Live*, a culinary guideline for physical and spiritual well-being. 'Not only does [eating the proper food] give us good health,' he wrote, 'but it gives us a better way of thinking, as food and our mental power work in the same way.'

Muhammad's call to plant-based eating was a direct response to the very factors that had disrupted the Indigenous Black diet in America more than 300 years prior: capitalism and racism. He suggested replacing processed foods with fresh fruits and vegetables, noting 'the food that we eat is robbed of its natural vitamins and proteins … for the sake of a commercial dollar.' He implored African Americans to break their bond with 'soul foods' that had been provided by Southern slave owners, citing physical and spiritual benefits. 'These foods destroy us,' he wrote of soul food. 'We are, by nature, vegetable- and fruit-eating people.'

The point of emphasis is to illustrate how an emergence of Black leaders and organizations later began to include a health focus as part of their organizational platform after the successful pronouncement and demonstration made by the Most Honorable Elijah Muhammad. This point is further acknowledged in two online articles I discovered. The first was published on July 2, 2014, by Jennifer Jensen Wallach, interestingly titled, "How to Eat to Live: Black Nationalism and the Post -1964 Culinary Turn."

> "Although the Nation of Islam had only about 20,000 members in 1966, the membership rolls alone do not capture the outsized influence the organization had on the black community. Most of the culinary nationalists of the era were heavily influenced by NOI teachings."

The second online source is from a book titled, "Hog and Hominy: Soul Food from Africa to America." It states the following:

"Before the 1980s, the Nation of Islam, more than any other African American organization, raised the food consciousness of black people in the United States."

When discussing the evolution of dietary habits of Black people, the late Dick Gregory's name is sure to come up at some point, and rightly so. **Dick Gregory,** born October 12, 1932, in St. Louis, Missouri, was an American comedian, civil rights activist, and spokesman for health issues. He became nationally recognized in the 1960s for a biting brand of comedy that attacked racial prejudice. By addressing his hard-hitting satire to white audiences, he gave a comedic voice to the rising civil rights movement.

In the 1980s, his nutrition business venture targeted unhealthy diets of Black Americans. When Dick Gregory's health transformation is reviewed, the name of another great leader in the field of health dietician, Dr. Alvenia Fulton, is often mentioned as being the catalyst for Mr. Gregory's full transformation. In a May

18, 2018, article found on the New York Public Library's website, written by A.J. Muhammad, titled, "Alvenia Fulton: A Pioneer in Health and Wellness Industry," it is stated:

"Fulton would later travel to the Midwest, where she earned degrees in nutrition and ultimately received a doctor of naturopathy degree. By the late 1950s, Fulton became a vegetarian and relocated to Chicago. From her home, she established and operated the Better Living Health Club where members learned how to lose weight and detox. The demands on the business were so great that Fulton outgrew her home work space and opened Fultonia's Health Food Center on Chicago's south side. With the help of a loan, she was able to renovate the space so patrons could get vegetarian meals, drinks from a juice bar, healthcare products, and advice from Fulton herself.

Word of mouth about Fulton and her knowledge of all things nutrition, dieting, and healthy living spread; soon, celebrities including Redd Foxx, Mahalia Jackson, Roberta Flack, Ruby Dee, Michael Caine, and Godfrey Cambridge came knocking.

In the 1960s, Fulton developed a long relationship with comedian and civil rights activist, Dick Gregory. Gregory consulted with Fulton regarding the many fasts he observed, including one that lasted for 54 days, to bring attention to causes such as racial and social injustice, and America's involvement in the war in Vietnam. In 1984, a News article reported that when Gregory signed a $100 million contract for the marketing rights to a product called Dick Gregory Slim Safe Bahamian Diet, Gregory granted $1 million each to a selection of charitable organizations, scholars, and others including Fulton 'to study fasting, hunger, starvation, malnutrition, and good nutrition.'"

While running for mayor of Chicago in 1967, Gregory met the nutritionist and naturopath Dr. Alvenia M. Fulton, who delivered a plate of greens to his campaign headquarters. The two struck up a lifelong friendship, with Fulton teaching Gregory to avoid animal protein and engage in fasting for longevity. As I read about the works of our dear sister, I found it remarkably interesting that she worked in Chicago teaching and promoting health at a time during the Nation of Islam's height. I immediately thought that she had to have had a connection or had been influenced by the Nation of Islam and the Teachings of How to Eat to Live. As I researched and read more, that thought was confirmed. The first piece of evidence that I found stating such was found in an article published in The Final Call newspaper covering the passing of Dick Gregory. The article is titled, "Dick Gregory Social satirist, teacher, activist and leader." It was written by Askia Muhammad, Charlene Muhammad, and Brian. The article states the following:

> "The strong influence of the Honorable Elijah Muhammad's teaching 'How To Eat To Live,' reached deep into all strata of life in Chicago, including to the work of dietician Dr. Alvenia Fulton who incorporated Mr. Muhammad's guidance into her work. Under treatment by Dr. Fulton, Mr. Gregory became a vegetarian, lost 50 pounds, embarked on a path where he even founded a diet product company, and he began to engage in extreme physical activities to support his activism."

Next, I came across an article titled, "Dick Gregory: Home to the Ancestors," by Gregg Reese on Aug 24, 2017, published in the Los Angeles Our Weekly. Mr. Reese states:

> "During his unsuccessful run for the Chicago mayoral spot, he made the acquaintance of Dr. Alvenia M. Fulton. An ordained minister affiliated with the Nation of Islam, she turned to naturopathic

medicine and dropped off some edibles at his campaign headquarters."

The impact and influence of the Most Honorable Elijah Muhammad is undeniable. It's puzzling that more is not discovered in the writings of Dick Gregory about the Most Honorable Elijah Muhammad's influence on his health transformation. Yes, there are some video recordings online where he speaks about the influence, but not in his writings. This oversight also caught the attention of Doris Witt, who wrote a chapter about Dick Gregory. This is written in a 2016 dissertation submitted to the Temple University Graduate Board by Heru Setepenra Heq-m-Ta, who states:

"It is a wonder how Elijah Muhammad's teachings and influence about health never made it into the discourse of Gregory's written words. In her telling, feminist treatise Black Hunger, Doris Witt's subtitle of chapter five, 'Dick Gregory's Cloacal Continuum' lends credence to Gregory's oversight in his writings. Witt explains it is quite interesting 'Gregory himself has little to say in his writings from this period about the Nation of Islam or its controversial leader [and] it seems possible that Gregory's indebtedness to Muhammad's dietary fixations is greater than he has been willing to admit. If his secular, integrationist politics are incompatible with Elijah Muhammad's advocacy of theistic [B]lack [N]nationalism, their dietary concerns share a number of striking similarities.' Paradoxically, for whatever the reason—be it his preceding theological and ideological variances—, later in life Dick Gregory acknowledges the ameliorative work of Elijah Muhammad in the same customary fashion as his naturalistic heroine Alvenia Fulton. For example, in the foreword to The Hood Health Handbook, Gregory, in reflection, reminisces about the 'Messenger's' nutritional call to arms to Blacks in the United States in a venerated manner: 'I can't help but think back to the great Elijah Muhammad, who talked about how diet is just as important as liberation.' In the same vein, in a one-on-one interview with Byron Hurt, the director of Soul Food Junkies, Gregory expresses the drastic impact Elijah Muhammad and the Nation of Islam had on the eating habits of many African Americans. Unapologetically, Gregory acknowledges to Hurt: 'The Biggest shock to me was what Elijah Muhammad was able to do with non-believers. My mother ain't gone be nothing but a Christian all her life, and would go to war if you told her...but she stop eating pork.' 'Why was that?' asked Hurt. Gregory's simple reply, without hesitation: 'Elijah Muhammad!' According to Gregory, no other theological organization had such a lasting impression and effect on the dietary ethics of African Americans like that of Elijah Muhammad and the Nation of Islam. Convincingly, Gregory upholds: 'I don't know anybody or a group of religious people that will never stop being anything but their religion but he got millions of black folks to stop eating pork. He wasn't our leader. He was their leader and we read the book and felt so comfortable with that we stopped eating pork.'

I pray that by now you are really beginning to see, on an even larger level, how extensive the influence of the Most Honorable Elijah Muhammad was and is. Yet, there is still more, as the Messenger of Allah was also an influence on another great giant in this area. I am referring to the late Dr. Sebi.

Born November 26th, 1933, in the village of Ilanga, Spanish Honduras, Dr. Sebi came into this world as Alfredo Bowman. Young Alfredo did not attend formal school; he was raised and educated by his cherished grandmother, Mama Hay, who influenced his understanding of nature that helped develop him into a great man and world-renowned herbalist.

Dr. Sebi's fascination with the natural world around him sparked a lifelong interest in the healing properties of plants. As a young man with asthma, diabetes, impotence and obesity, Dr. Sebi was drawn to natural healing methods, especially after discovering firsthand the limitations of Western medicine in treating chronic disease. Dr. Sebi studied herbs in Africa, the Caribbean, North America, and Central and South America. In Mexico, he met an herbalist who alleviated all of his health complaints and explained to him that being from Africa, he should follow an original African diet! Inspired by the mighty healing potential of herbs, Dr. Sebi went on to create natural vegetation cell food compounds that clean and replenish the body, the first prototypes of *Dr. Sebi's Cell Food.*

Dedicating his life to the pursuit of natural, plant-based approaches for health management and disease prevention, Dr. Sebi treated high profile clientele, including Michael Jackson, Eddie Murphy, John Travolta, Lisa "Left Eye" Lopes of TLC, and Teddy Pendergrass, and his efforts continue to enrich the health and wellbeing of millions of people around the world.

Dr. Sebi passed away in 2016, leaving a legacy of natural healing knowledge, philosophy and wisdom that is our duty to pass onto future generations for the healing of all humankind.

There are online interviews where Dr. Sebi talks about the influence of the Most Honorable Elijah Muhammad on his life.

"I was a Muslim! Ya know? I was in Islam. I love Islam! Islam gave me a whole lot of good things. I mean I met Elijah Muhammad. I met the Messenger. I was talking to him like I am talking to you. But the Messenger's information at the time needed a little more help. So, he told me I could not eat meat any longer, the lamb. I could not drink any milk. I abstained from all of these things and here I am at 82." *(Rock Newman Show)*

"Our Honorable Elijah Muhammad, the only man that said stay away from the pork. And when I, Sebi, sat and ate with the Messenger in his house on 3837 South Woodlawn in Chicago, the Messenger personally told me and Brother Harry Nance from New Orleans that we should not be eating meat at all, and we should not be eating anything on this menu..." *(Instagram video clip posted by Brother Ben X)*

The above words from Dr. Sebi himself show that he had contact with Islam and admitted he was a Muslim. What he learned from that body of knowledge gave him "a whole lot of good things." In addition to that, he acknowledges that he met with and was taught by the Most Honorable Elijah Muhammad. For those who may still question such, I would like to provide a transcript by an interview conducted by Rizza Islam with Dr. Akili Muhammad, who is a medical physician. The interview can be found on YouTube on the Ultimate Wellness Group page under the video titled, "How to Eat to Live and Dr. Sebi."

Brother Rizza Islam: Wow, wow, wow, wow. Okay, so that's from veganism, eating raw vs. cooked. Wow, okay. And from your perspective, there's something you mentioned as well, because our brother, our now ancestor Brother Dr. Sebi, may Allah be pleased with him, beautiful work, and beautiful brother. Where is it, because a lot of people say it's controversial. Where is it that he received his initial knowledge from when he started his journey on health and learning about foods and vegetables? Where did he get that information from, in the beginning?

Dr. Akili Muhammad: Yes sir, excellent question. First let me say to everybody that I am not talking about gossip, hearsay. I ain't talking about something I read. I sat with this man side by side on a 4-hour trip, plane trip, from Houston to Philadelphia the first time I met him, and we talked the entire trip. So I'm not telling you what I heard from somebody else. I'm not interpreting anything. This is what this man told me person-to-person. He lived in New York. His wife got sick. He left his house to go find the answers to how to help his wife. When he left his house, he said he ran into some brothers. They were in the Nation of Islam, and they told him that he needed to get "How to Eat to Live." He bought "How to Eat to Live," and at the same time he got that book, he was turned on to a Chinese herbalist. And so between some soup that the Chinese herbalist gave him and told him how to make and "How to Eat to Live" is where Dr. Sebi got his start when it came to health. He said he studied "How to Eat to Live." He said he studied it and studied it and studied it for years.

Rizza Islam: Yes sir.

Dr. Akili Muhammad: When he saw that "How to Eat Live" was helping his wife get better, he said that he wanted to research it and be able to prove what was in this book helping his wife. So again, these are the words that Dr. Sebi was telling me personally, and so Dr. Sebi is somebody that I greatly respect. Dr. Sebi is somebody that I learned a lot from, but my total passion and my total commitment is to this book, because as a physician, I left that world of hospitals and institutions that are just putting our people on medications and keeping them sick. I left that when this showed me that this can solve people's problems, help people cure problems. And so my assessment of what Dr. Sebi did was, he left from "How to Eat to Live" and then went started learning other things, and this started compiling things which produced his program. He did great. This is not a detriment to talk. This is not to try to put him down, but I don't agree or go with some of the things that he taught, because they go against this book, which is where he got his foundation. So this is a clarifying discussion about Dr. Sebi. I hope that nobody takes this as somebody trying to slight his name, trying to throw shade on the brother. That's not what I'm about. I don't do those type of things. I would rather not talk about him, and I'm not one to sit back and be half-cocked and I'm gonna talk about you, I'm gonna talk about you. So if I had something negative to say, about time to say, me, I would say it. I don't, I just am clarifying for people that talk about what Dr. Sebi had as a dietary, but when we talked about certain foods that you do eat and you don't eat it, not this way, you cook this and this is bad. If that man right there said it from "How to Eat to Live" what another person..."

Today, more than ever, we are seeing more Black people taking charge of their health. Every one of the people we mentioned in this chapter have played a role in this work, including others who are not mentioned. We thank Allah and applaud them for their service.

We are happy that we are seeing more of our people look for other alternatives to the traditional "soul food" diet that is so popular and unhealthy. Yes, Black people are still suffering from poor health choices and habits, but we are witnessing a growth, which means there has and is a mental elevation taking place. We are working to ensure that the Most Honorable Elijah Muhammad's impact, role and influence is not left out. When the history is written regarding the transformation of Black people in America's eating habits, the name of the Most Honorable Elijah Muhammad MUST be included, for he is the one the Qur'an speaks of who will teach the People of God what to eat and what to store in their houses.

CHAPTER 7
Clarence 13X: Another Fruit from the Tree

To refer to the Most Honorable Elijah Muhammad as a Master Teacher is an accurate statement, because he has produced and continues to produce a cadre of impactful students. This chapter provides further evidence.

In this chapter, we want to cover the history of another great student of the Most Honorable Elijah Muhammad who was awakened by the Teachings and who went out into the streets and began a community that still exists today. That student is Clarence 13X, known by his followers as Father Allah. To help with accurately presenting his history and accomplishments, I want to rely on research by another Nation of Islam historian, Brother Wakeel Allah, who wrote a book about Clarence 13X titled, "In the Name of Allah, Volume 1: A History of Clarence 13X and the Five Percenters." In an article published in The

Final Call newspaper, Brother Wakeel wrote the following:

"The historical ties between the Nation of Islam and the Five Percenters date back to the latter's very inception. After returning to Harlem from the Korean War and his stint in the Army, Clarence 13X Smith a.k.a. Allah, the founder of the Five Percenters, followed his wife Dora and his family into the Nation of Islam under the leadership of the Honorable Elijah Muhammad and local Temple No. 7 Minister Malcolm X in 1960.

In the N.O.I. he became Clarence 13X and joined the Fruit of Islam under Captain Yusef Shah and became immersed into the discipline and teachings of the Hon. Elijah Muhammad where he learned to recite his lessons, served on security details, field maneuvers, sold Muhammad Speaks newspapers and worked as a painter for Muslim-owned Earth Painters Improvement Company. Within the N.O.I. he became close companions with John 37X (Abu Shahid) and James 109X (4 Cipher Akbar, Justice), as well as taught a young teen he named Hebekah while out selling the paper on 125th Street. Clarence soldiered in the F.O.I. from 1960-1964, and exited the Mosque in 1964, where he witnessed the historic case of the teens known as 'The Harlem Six' and the Blood Brothers who were heavily influenced by N.O.I. speeches on street corners by Min. Malcolm X. After the arrest of the Harlem Six, Bro. Clarence and his above mentioned protégés formerly of the mosque invented the lesson Supreme Mathematics which they derived from

Problem Number 13 in 'The Problem Book' of the Nation of Islam, and started teaching neighborhood youth they labeled as the Five Percenters. Clarence changed his name to 'Allah' and taught his young followers the dietary laws and lessons of the Hon. Elijah Muhammad, and had his original students who later came to be known as 'the First Borns' listening to the Sunday radio broadcasts of the Hon. Elijah Muhammad.

In the beginning phases, Allah was harassed by the police and arrested for 'disturbing the peace' while having a rally in front of the Hotel Theresa in Harlem. He later was sentenced to Mattewan Hospital for almost 2 years for his involvement in the Five Percenters. In his absence, the Elders and Firstborns kept teaching the lessons to other youth, and the Five Percenters spread throughout New York City.

Upon his release from prison, Allah held his first 'Universal Parliament' in Mt. Morris Park to teach the 5 Percenters. In attendance was Min. Akbar Muhammad (former Larry 4X) who spoke with Clarence about the work he was doing with the youth. Not long afterwards, the mayor of New York John Lindsay started working with the Five Percenters in regard to having them take advantage of city and state programs such as opening up a street academy which happened in 1967. At the same time the Five Percenters adopted a new 'Universal Flag' that consisted of the 7, Sun, Crescent Moon and 8 pointed star. The 7 stood for 'God' and the planets represented 'Knowledge, Wisdom, Understanding, Man, Woman and Child, and Master Fard Muhammad, the Honorable Elijah Muhammad and Allah.'

On June 13, 1969, Clarence 13X was assassinated by unknown assailants. The Five Percenters survived the assassination by keeping the lessons alive and spreading them to other youth. The Five Percenters also became pioneers within rap and Hip-Hop culture and became prominent within the genre boasting of many celebrities in the genre today including the World Famous Supreme Team, Rakim, Big Daddy Kane, Poor Righteous Teachers, Brand Nubian, Digable Planets, Busta Rhymes, Erykah Badu, the Wu-Tang Clan and many others. Most have established relationships with the Hon. Min. Louis Farrakhan and the Nation of Islam.

Today the Five Percenters (Gods and Earths) and Nation of Islam still have an intertwined legacy as many Muslims in the ranks today got their start in the Five Percent Nation including New York's N.O.I. Representative Abdul Hafeez Muhammad of Mosque #7, Historian of

Cover from the book: In The Name of Allah; A History of Clarence 13X And The Five Percenters

religion and aide to the Honorable Minister Louis Farrakhan Dr. Wesley Muhammad, Record Producer Haqq Islam, authors Shahid M. Allah (Jay Muhammad), celebrity rap entertainer Jay Electronica and myself. Five Percent Nation tradition says that Father Allah instructed that some of the Five Percenters would return to the ranks of the Nation of Islam, and that they 'would have a job to do there, and a job to do here.' Whatever be the case, both the Nation of Islam and the Five Percenters (Nation of Gods and Earths) continue down the path of supporting the mission of resurrecting Black people and teaching all the human families of the planet Earth, which is the 'one common cause' of 'Freedom, Justice and Equality for all.'"

Brother Clarence 13X used the Supreme Wisdom Lessons, which contains instructions by the Teacher of the Most Honorable Elijah Muhammad and Founder of the Nation of Islam, Master Fard Muhammad. The Supreme Wisdom also has the answers of the Most Honorable Elijah Muhammad, which every Registered Member of the Nation of Islam are instructed to commit to memory. Brother Clarence 13X used this knowledge to teach the youth he encountered in the streets of New York, and he developed the Supreme Alphabets and Supreme Mathematics. Decades later, the impact of this student of the Most Honorable Elijah Muhammad is being felt all over America and the world!

If we remove the Most Honorable Elijah Muhammad, Black America and the many youths who were touched by Brother Clarence 13X would have not been impacted, for the basis upon which

Brother Clarence 13X made the Supreme Mathematics and Alphabet came from the Lessons of the Most Honorable Elijah Muhammad.

Brother Clarence 13X never lost his admiration for the Most Honorable Elijah Muhammad and his leadership. This is evident based upon what Brother Clarence 13X told one of his top students before he was killed. In Brother Wakeel's book, "In the Name of Allah, Vol. 2," he includes this excerpt from an interview with Rasul, also known as Hebekah, where Father Allah said that if something were to happen to him, they should return back to the Temple.

"Nobody really could take the Father place and I knew it. Shahid didn't try to take his place. You know, you got brothers now, they doing this, they doing that. They would have never done one of that at that time. They would have never did that—they would have never did that. He never taught us to take over the community. The only thing I heard him say was, 'Go with Elijah.' I never heard him say nothing else. He never told me to go with Justice, go with Shahid or nobody. Never."

Brother Wakeel includes another discussion where the same sentiment was expressed.

"Rasul (Hebekah) recalls another night when Allah stated this emphatically: 'He said, he told us, that night, he said, 'My man, if something happened to me...' He didn't say we had to, he said, 'If I was you-I would go join Elijah.' And his reason was that he said, 'Because Elijah loves his people.' That's what he told us.'"

We honor the work of Brother Clarence 13X. The Honorable Minister Louis Farrakhan has publicly praised his work and praised the 5 Percenters. They are our family, and we wish them the best of success.

CHAPTER 8
The Honorable Elijah Muhammad's Impact on Hip-Hop

I did a Google search on the following, "Hip-Hop Lyrics About Elijah Muhammad." There were over one million results. I open this chapter stating that to show how the Teachings of the Most Honorable Elijah Muhammad have held a very significant place in the music and culture of hip-hop and its "Conscious Era."

In an article titled "Is It Nation of Islam Time Again in Hip-Hop," Zaheer Ali writes:

> "In the late '80s and early '90s, a wave of commercial hip-hop artists, like Public Enemy, Poor Righteous Teachers, Brand Nubian, Eric B. & Rakim, Paris, Gang Starr, Ice Cube and MC Ren, used their platform to promote political awareness, community uplift and cultural self-determination. They drew their inspiration in part from Islam—as culture, ideology and religion—influenced primarily by the Nation of Islam and its offshoot the Nation of Gods and Earths, or Five Percenters."

This historical fact is also acknowledged in a GQ article titled, "How Islam Inspired Hip Hop." Journalist Nooriyah Qais states:

"But the influence of Islam on African-American culture dates well before the rise of hip-hop in the Bronx, and to a time when Malcolm X, Muhammed Ali, and the Nation of Islam particularly influenced the Black culture in seeking an identity that could ultimately resist oppression.

'These movements shaped the political consciousness for Black people who were searching for a cultural identity,' explains educator and former editor-in-chief of The Source, Fahiym Abdul-Wasi. 'Religion played a part in that, with Black [communities] who felt that Christianity was, quote, unquote, the white man's religion. Islam, for a lot of Black people, represented the religion of our ancestors and became very big from the 1950s. The Nation of Islam was the movement that put Islam on the map in terms of the national consciousness for a lot of people and that has had a big effect on early hip-hop.'

Hip-hop emerged at a time that spoke to many people about social issues that Islam has historically regarded as well. Things like inequity, self-determination and the need for national community or an ummah. This directly influenced hip-hop culture as a whole and was reflected in lyrics via mentions of Malcolm X and Louis Farrakhan (Nation of Islam leader since 1977). Artists were studying Islam, applying it to their daily lives, and spreading the word to help build a nation."

All of this can be accredited to a Georgia-born Black man who was raised by his Teacher in Detroit, the Most Honorable Elijah Muhammad. He produced students that touched the minds of Black youth all throughout America, especially in New York, which is regarded as the "Home of Hip-Hop" or the "Mecca of Hip-Hop."

DJ Kook Herc and Afrika Bambaataa are considered some of the founding fathers of Hip-Hop. Clive Campbell, born April 16, 1955, better known by his stage name DJ Kool Herc, is a Jamaican-born American DJ who is credited with originating hip-hop music in the mid-1970s in The Bronx, New York City. His playing of hard funk records of the sort typified by James Brown was an alternative to the violent gang culture of the Bronx and the nascent popularity of disco in the 1970s. Campbell began to isolate the instrumental portion of the record, which emphasized the drumbeat - the "break" - and switch from one break to another to another.

Using the same two turntable set-up of disco DJs, Campell used two copies of the same record to lengthen the break. This breakbeat DJing, using hard funk, rock, and Latin percussion records, formed the basis of hip-hop music. Campbell's announcements and exhortations to dancers helped lead to the syncopated, rhymed spoken accompaniment now known as rapping. He called his dancers "break-boys" and "break-girls", or simply, b-boys and b-girls. Campbell's DJ style influenced figures such as Afrika Bambaataa and Grandmaster Flash. Unlike them, he never made the move into commercially recorded hip-hop and has not released any albums.

West Indian hip-hop legend Afrika Bambaataa (Kevin Donovan) was born October 4, 1957, and grew up in the South Bronx, New York. A huge lover of music, Bam collected R&B and rock records and played trumpet and piano while attending Adlai E. Stevenson High School. Taking the name of a 19th century Zulu chief, Bambaataa joined the local Bronx Rivers Projects division of the notorious Black Spades street gang. Though neighborhood violence was common during the early 1970s, a new form of music called hip-hop and block parties helped ease community tensions. As gang popularity began to diminish in 1973, Bam soon found himself break-beat DJing at house parties after being inspired by DJ Kool Herc and Kool DJ Dee. His catalog not only included typical R&B and Funk records, but also consisted of atypical genres like Go-Go, Soca, Salsa Reggae, Rock, Jazz, Funk and African music.

DJ Afrika Bambaataa easily drew party crowds with the help of his former

Black Spade following, but he soon realized that his true passion was to unify urban youth through his newly formed group called the Universal Zulu Nation. Bam referred to the movement, culture and music as "Hip Hop," and it became the tool he used to draw kids away from the perils of gang life. His definition of the culture included the elements of MCing, DJing, B-boying, graffiti, and knowledge.

Both of these foundational figures of hip-hop were impacted by Islam, specifically, the Islam as taught by the Most Honorable Elijah Muhammad, though not always explicitly stated. The article, "A brief history of Islam and hip-hop, from DJ Kool Herc to Alia Sharrief," reads:

> "What's perhaps less well known is that two out of three of them – Kool and Afrika – personally studied the teachings of the Five-Percent Nation, a movement influenced by Islam. They incorporated enough of these studies into the genre to prompt Professor Felicia M Miyakawa to write a book on the subject in 2005, *Five Percenter Rap: God's Hop Music, Message and the Black Muslim Mission.*"

There are other hip-hop historians who are more forthright about the influences of the Teachings of the Most Honorable Elijah Muhammad, as seen in the article, "Hip-hop's little known companion: Event shows fans hip-hop and Islam connection," by Janiah Adams. In the article, she interviews Tony Muhammad.

> "Tony Muhammad, a member of the Nation of Islam and public-school teacher, said DJ Kool Herc, who's considered to be the founding father of hip-hop culture, was affiliated with the Nation of Gods and Earths, otherwise known as the 5 Percenters, an Islamic group started by a former member of the Nation of Islam.
>
> '[Kool Herc] is known as the father of hip-hop because he started up the first hip-hop party in the South Bronx,' Muhammad said. 'With him, a lot of times you would see him wearing a shirt with the Nation of Gods and Earths' insignia on it – the universal flag.' Muhammad said much of the colloquialisms that were used in the Nation of Islam, such as 'your word is your bond,' were used among young people. Artists such as Rakim and LL Cool J used the phrase in their songs."

Hisham Aidi is the author of a book titled, "Rebel Music: Race, Empire, and the New Muslim Youth Culture." In an online article titled, "'Rebel Music': When Hip-Hop Met Islam," the writer says the following regarding the influence that Islam—specifically taught by the Most Honorable Elijah Muhammad—had on Afrika Bambaataa and his musical genius.

"Aidi says he researched the way that jazz, R&B and other American styles have extended beyond the country's borders, and found that the richest cross-fertilization between American music and Islam is found in hip-hop — beginning in the early 1970s with hip-hop pioneer Afrika Bambaataa his cultural awareness group the Zulu Nation.

'They emerge in 1973. They form the Zulu Nation to combat street violence. And they begin to draw on Nation of Islam teachings and the texts that Muslims believe,' he says. 'And then in the early '80s, you begin to get references to Malcolm X, and eventually these references make their way into some hip hop classics — the works of Rakim and Public Enemy and so on.'"

Hip-hop journalist and historian Davey D. interviewed Afrika Bambaataa on a different occasion.

"A few weeks ago I had the pleasure of speaking to a living legend, **Afrika Bambaataa**, whose innovativeness and love for hip hop has permanently impacted pop culture. During our in-depth 2 hour conversation, Bam gave some serious insight into rap music. He went into detail about the formation of his organization The Zulu Nation. He told how they were former gang members who reformed and channeled their energies into breakdancing. He told how the emergence of hip hop culture helped curtail gang violence in NY because it offered young people a viable activity.

Bam also spoke about the inherent politicalness in hip hop. He told how the **Nation Of Islam** had influenced him and others during the 'old school' [1975-1980]. He also spoke about his activism."

The influence of Islam as taught by the Most Honorable Elijah Muhammad did not stop with the two founders of this genre, which has become the most impactful musical art form in the world. MANY (I capitalize that word intentionally), of the great lyrical giants of the world of hip-hop were also either Muslims and/or influenced by guess what? The Teachings of the Most Honorable Elijah Muhammad!

Rakim, considered to be one of the greatest lyricists of all time, was one of the earliest hip-hop artists to incorporate references to Islam into his work. Born William Griffin, he later became a Five Percenter, adopting the name Rakim Allah. In Rakim's song, "The Ghetto," he raps about the history of the Caucasian after they were exiled from the Roots of Civilization.

> "Called and go back to the essence
> It's a lot to learn so I study my lessons
> I thought the ghetto was the worst that could happen to me. I'm glad I listen when my father was rapping to me. 'Cause back in the days, they lived in caves. Exile from the original man, a straight way Now that's what I call hard times. I rather be here to exercise the mind..."

This history can be easily read in the monumental book, Message to the Blackman in America by the Most Honorable Elijah Muhammad, in the chapter titled, "The Making of the Devil.'

> "Yakub's made devils were driven out of Paradise, into the hills of West Asia (Europe), and stripped of everything but the language. They walked across that hot, sandy desert, into the land where long

years of both trouble and joy awaited them; but --
they finally made it. (Not all: many died in the
desert.) Once there, they were roped in, to keep
them out of Paradise. To make sure, the Muslims,
who lived along the borders of East and West Asia,
were ordered to patrol the border to keep Yakub's
devils in West Asia (now called Europe), so that the
original nation of black man could live in peace; and
the devils could be alone to themselves, to do as
they pleased, as long as they didn't try crossing the
East border. The soldiers patrolled the border
armed with swords, to prevent the devils from
crossing. This went on for 2,000 years. After that
time, Musa (Moses) was born: the man whom Allah
would send to these exiled devils to bring them
again into the light of civilization. Before we take up
this first 2,000 years of the devils exiled on our
planet, let us not lose sight of what and how they
were made, and of the god who made them, Mr.
Yakub..."

Mr. Muhammad continues to explain the savage condition they fell into.

"Yakub's race of devils were exiled in the hills and
caves of West Asia (now called Europe). They were
without anything to start civilization and became
savages. They remained in such condition for 2,000
years--no guide or literature. They lost all
knowledge of civilization. The Lord, God of Islam,
taught me that some of them tried to graft
themselves back into the black nation, but they had
nothing to go by. A few were lucky enough to make
a start, and got as far as what you call the gorilla. In

fact, all of the monkey family are from this 2,000 year history of the white race in Europe. Being deprived of divine guidance for their disobedience, the making of mischief and causing bloodshed in the holy nation of the original black people by lies, they became so savage that they lost all their sense of shame. They started going nude as they are doing today (and leading the so-called Negroes into the very acts). They became shameless. In the winter they wore animal skins for clothes and grew hair all over their bodies and faces like all the other wild animals. In those days, they made their homes in the caves on hillsides. There is a whole chapter devoted to them in the Holy Qur'an. They had it very hard, trying to save themselves from being destroyed by wild beasts which were plentiful at that time in Europe. Being without a guide, they started walking on their hands and feet like all animals; and, learned to climb trees as well as any of the animals. At night, they would climb up into trees, carrying large stones and clubs, to fight the wild beasts that would come prowling around at night, to keep them from eating their families. Their next and best weapons were the dogs. They tamed some of these dogs to live in the caves with their families, to help protect them from the wild beasts. After a time, the dog held a high place among the family because of his fearlessness to attack the enemies of his master. Today, the dog is still loved by the white race and is given more justice than the so-called Negroes, and, is called the white man's best friend. This comes from the cave days."

Even Jay-Z, who is considered to be "The GOAT (the Greatest of All Time) of Hip-Hop," references this aspect of the Teachings of the Most Honorable Elijah Muhammad in a remix with him and Jay Electronica titled, "Ni***as We Made It!" Jay-Z raps:

> "I'm God, G is the seventh letter made.
> So when my arms and feet shackled I still get paid
> All praises due. I'm ready to chase the Yakub back
> into caves..."

In Rakim's album, the 18th Letter there is a song titled, "The Mystery (Who is God?)." The track's title itself reflects the very foundational truth the Most Honorable Elijah Muhammad said he was taught by Allah to dispel from the minds of Black people, which is the belief that God is a mystery, as stated in the opening chapter of Message to the Blackman in the chapter titled, "Allah is God Who is that Mystery God?"

> "Today, the God of Truth and Righteousness is making Himself manifest, that He is not anymore a mystery (unknown), but is known and can be seen and heard the earth over. This teaching of a mystery

God enslaves the minds of the ignorant. My poor people are victims of every robbery. They are so pitifully blind, deaf and dumb that it hurts, but I am going to prove to them that I am with Allah (God) and that Allah is with me, in spite of their ignorance of Allah and myself, whom He has sent. For I am not self-sent and the world shall soon know who it is that has sent me. Allah (God) loves us, the so-called Negroes (Tribe of Shabazz,) so that He will give lives for our sake today. Fear not, you are no more forsaken."

The God MC, Rakim, goes in on this track, dropping more of the jewels about God that was brought to the Black man and woman in America, by Allah (God) Himself, in the Person of Master Fard Muhammad. One of the jewels Master Fard Muhammad revealed is how Allah (God) the Originator Self-created Himself. Rakim uses his lyrical skill coupled with the knowledge of the Teachings to artfully articulate this truth to his listeners.

"If you can see if you can solve the mystery.
The answer revolves around your history.
So carefully. I drop this degree. Scientifically and realistically (Who is God?) In eternal blackness in the midst of the darkest night. Proteins and minerals exist within specks of light. Solids liquids and gases and sparks of light within. Infinite lengths

and widths and depths and heights. No beginning or ending, the seven dimensions. Enough space for more than a million words and inventions. To travel through time within enough room to be the womb. Of the most high's great mind which he will soon make shine. With intelligent elements in sight that he will gather. In the realms of relativity electricity struck matter. Energies explode he below to keep releasin. Atoms by the millions, til the numbers increasin. Til it was burnin he kept returnin itself to the source. The hotter his thoughts it gave the center more force. He gave birth to the sun which would follow his laws. All caused by his mental intercourse, who is God?"

The Most Honorable Elijah Muhammad's Number One student, the Honorable Minister Louis Farrakhan, explained this trillions-of-years-old Secret of God in a historic lectured titled, "The Knowledge of God."

"I want to go back to God being 'not begotten.' The Holy Qur'an says, 'He begets not, nor is He begotten.' The Muslims say this is why God could never be a human being, because all human beings are 'begotten.'

I want you to follow this very carefully. The Honorable Elijah Muhammad taught us that before there was a sun, moon and star, before there was light, God was Self-Created. God created Himself out of the material of darkness. Before there was anything, there was darkness, but it was a substantive darkness. What we see at night is not real darkness. It is called the absence of light because we are just in the shadow of the Earth. We live in a Universe of Light, where once there was total darkness. But matter was in the darkness. Even though matter was in the darkness, it is considered nothing, because it was without aim and purpose. Anything without aim and purpose is considered nothing.

The Honorable Elijah Muhammad taught us that electricity is the most mysterious force because no one knows its origin. When you have electricity and matter in the darkness, you can produce the first germ of life. Whatever happened with electricity and matter, the first atom of life sparked in the darkness. There is intelligence in the life-germ. Our own beginning bears witness to the beginning of the Universe. The very secret of how the Universe began is wrapped up in how you and I began.

You don't know the Universe, because you don't know God, because you don't know yourself.

Look at the sperm. There is intelligence in the sperm; it knows exactly what it wants to do: it goes straight for the egg; that is intelligence. The sperm does not have a brain, but it has a head and a tail. When the sperm makes contact, it's the first cell of life. That cell starts looking for a firm resting place, then it builds a clot. There is intelligence in that clot. Then the cells produce brain. That's the first thing formed in the new life. Without a head, you don't need arms. The thing that is going to direct the arms has to be first. It is the head that calls the arms and feet into existence.

This is why the white man works to destroy your leaders. Without a head, you cannot call a body into existence. That is why you are always without organization: you never have leadership. Your leadership comes up and when they spot it as good leadership, they wipe it out.

The Honorable Elijah Muhammad taught us that God had to develop brain in order to think through darkness. It took pain and eons of time for God to build Himself up in the darkness. He was Light of Himself and had Light in Himself. Since the basis of His Life is electricity, He had Light in Himself. From His own Brain, He envisioned Sun and then called it into existence.

The Honorable Elijah Muhammad said Allah formed Himself, not from a mother, but out of the dark womb of space. Space and the darkness of it became His womb and He came out of that darkness."

Rakim's music is filled with the Teachings, and what we have highlighted is just a scratch of the surface, if that. Rakim is only one whose lyrics we highlighted. This chapter can go on and on if we showed the presence and impact of the Teachings of the Most Honorable Elijah Muhammad on the following limited number of artists: Big Daddy Kane, Paris, Ice Cube, Busta Rhymes, Public Enemy, Wu Tang Clan, Nas, Poor Righteous Teachers, Doug E. Fresh, Brand Nubians, Jay Electronica, Digable Planets, etc. The list can go on and on. However, there is no need to run, because by now, beyond a shadow of a doubt, you should be able to CLEARLY see the influence of a man, who some are trying to write out of history, on this powerful genre of rap.

In closing, an argument could be made that the overabundance of Gangster Rap was intentionally planned as a way to counter the impact and the presence of the Nation of Islam and other conscious thought leaders for the purpose of keeping the masses, especially Black people, deaf, dumb and blind. That subject is a book in itself.

CHAPTER 9
His Number One Student

One of the major figures that has greatly thwarted this effort to write the Most Honorable Elijah Muhammad out of history is his Number One Student, the Honorable Minister Louis Farrakhan. I do not use the label, "Number One Student" without the evidence historically and scripturally to support that statement of FACT! It is not a subjective statement at all! It is, as I stated, a FACT!

I am a veteran educator. I have taught in various school systems throughout my career and have positively touched the hearts and minds of many students in my time, by Allah's Permission. One thing I know from my experience as an educator is that one of the methods by which the knowledge, the understanding, the application and a student's mastery of covered content is assessed is through some form of a test. The Most Honorable Elijah Muhammad and the Honorable Minister Louis Farrakhan, as well as many of the other ministers and laborers of the Most Honorable Elijah Muhammad, had a teacher and student relationship. The Most Honorable Elijah Muhammad tested them all, from Malcolm X and Muhammad Ali to Warith Deen Mohammed and the Honorable Minister Louis Farrakhan. Out of them, the Honorable Minister Louis Farrakhan successfully passed many of the tests! This is not just my opinion but also words spoken by the Most Honorable Elijah Muhammad to the Minister and to others. God-willing, we will do our best to show as much of this as we can by first showing the words the Most Honorable Elijah Muhammad shared about his student, the tests that the Honorable Minister Louis Farrakhan passed, the attempts the Minister resisted to get him to stop teaching about his Teacher in the forms of bribes and even threats on his life, and the work the Minister has been doing in the name of his teacher before and after 1975. God-willing, we will close out with those words by the Most Honorable Elijah Muhammad about the Minister passing these tests.

NOI Researcher Brother Demetric Muhammad in the book, "An Invincible Truth: The Most Honorable Elijah Muhammad's Pittsburgh Courier Articles Collection," includes the following words from the Most Honorable Elijah Muhammad about the Honorable Minister Louis Farrakhan.

"Throughout the years of the close teacher-student relationship between the Most Honorable Elijah Muhammad and the Honorable Minister Louis Farrakhan, there are several statements and declarations made by the Honorable Elijah Muhammad that we now cite for the benefit of the reader.

Elijah Muhammad Says, Farrakhan Is Best Helper

Allah couldn't have given me a better helper... They can't help but to follow a man like that! Got the whole big city New York all stirred up!...

If I was all the other Ministers, I'd take pattern [after him]. Like the Disciples did Paul. Paul was one of the greatest preachers the Disciples had. Well, he wasn't one of the Disciples, but he came up and beat all the other disciples...

Source: Sultan R. Muhammad, Table Talks of the Honorable Elijah Muhammad - The Transcripts: Volume One, Second, ed. Table Talks Project Editorial Board (Chicago, IL: ICJ Press, 2013).

Elijah Muhammad Says, Farrakhan Puts Everything In Its Proper Place

The Hon. Elijah Muhammad (THEM): Well, my Brother Minister [Farrakhan], you've got a lot of things lined up in the right and the most best way.

Minister Louis Farrakhan (MLF): Thank you, Dear Apostle.

THEM: I love to see you wise because that gives me pleasure because I'm your teacher...and I made such wise ministers.

Group of Ministers: Yes, Sir!

Dr. Salaam (DS): Yes, you gave birth to all of us.
THEM: So when I see you acting and speaking wise I have rejoice in my heart. I say this is the ONE (i.e. MLF) the world can't bother. I want to prove to Satan that my minister is a greater light to the world of man than you and your world's man—the whole of them.

MLF: Yes sir. Bless you Dear Apostle.

THEM: It's wonderful.

THEM: Well, that's what I'm saying I can sit here and listen to you (MLF) and then I can step back and smile. I just need you to be Paul, you know. Go ahead on and put it out just like you are doing. You'll put it out, sometimes I sit here— we all sit here and get a chance to listen at you, I listen at you brother, preaching Brother, and you'll be surprised just to take a peek at the room through your spiritual eye and look at us. We enjoy it!

MLF: All praises due to Allah.

THEM: You [MLF] put everything in such proper place wherein it belongs. It' s beautiful! So we all is very happy over you, from Allah—that Allah made a helper.

Source: Sultan R Muhammad, Table Talks of the Honorable Elijah Muhammad - The Transcripts: Volume One, Second, ed. Table Talks Project Editorial Board (Chicago, IL: MUI Press, December 1973, 2012).

Elijah Muhammad Says, Continue To Hear Farrakhan

"I want you to remember, today I have one of my greatest teachers here. We have with us today our great national preacher. The preacher who don't mind going into Harlem, New York, one of the worst towns in our nation or cities. He is our brother in Detroit or Chicago or New York.

I want you to remember, every week he's on the air helping me reach those people that I can't get out of the house. I want you to pay good attention to his preaching. His preaching is a bearing of witness to me and what God has given me.

This is one of the strongest national preachers that I have in the bounds of North America. Everywhere you hear him listen to him. Everywhere you see him, look at him. Everywhere he advises you to go, go. Everywhere he advises you to stay from, stay from.

So, we are thankful to Allah for this great helper of mine, Minister Farrakhan. He's not a proud man. He's a very humble man. If he can carry you across the lake without dropping you in, he doesn't say when he gets on the other side, 'See what I have done?' He tells you, 'See what Allah has done.' He doesn't take it upon himself.

He's a mighty fine preacher. We hear him every week and I say, continue to hear our Minister Farrakhan.

Source: Elijah Muhammad, 'The Theology of Time (Lecture Series),' Vols. July 30, 1972 (Chicago, IL: MUHAMMAD Mosque No. 2, 1972).

Elijah Muhammad Says, Farrakhan Full of Allah's Spirit

"You know, Brother Farrakhan is a very good minister. He has been with us for a long time and he's a man full of fire. The fire of the Holy Spirit of Allah. Wonderful minister, wonderful."

Source: Elijah Muhammad, 'The Theology of Time (Lecture Series),' Vols. July 16, 1972 (Chicago, IL: MUHAMMAD Mosque No. 2, 1972).

These excerpts are a few of the many that support my position of Minister Farrakhan being Elijah Muhammad's valedictorian. And the Minister's value to the Most Honorable Elijah Muhammad must be acknowledged as the highest of honors conferred upon the Minister."

Ask those who argue that the Honorable Minister Louis Farrakhan is not the Number One Student of the Most Honorable Elijah Muhammad, or as Brother Demetric states, "Elijah Muhammad's valedictorian," to show another student the Most Honorable Elijah Muhammad spoke such words about?

The Honorable Minister Louis Farrakhan, when he was Louis X, a newly registered member of the Nation of Islam, was tested when the order from the Most

Honorable Elijah Muhammad came down telling his followers who were in the music industry to leave it or leave the Nation. Minister Farrakhan, only months in the Nation, did not bat an eye! He shared this experience in Part 7 of his historic 58-part series titled, 'The Time and What Must Be Done."

"I was living in New York at the time in 1955, so when I got back to New York, I went to the Temple No. 7 and heard Malcolm X. Well, 'that was it': I had never heard a Black man speak like that! And by this time, it was the summer, and since I had not heard back about my Letter I wrote in February in Chicago, I took my form out and wrote my Letter again, and it was accepted around the first week of October of that year.

Being a musician and wanting to go back to Boston and deliver that Message: I never knew that I had the 'gift of speech.' However, on a Wednesday evening, Brother Malcolm asked for the new converts to come and have a word to say, and when he called 'Louis X' up, he said: *'I'd like you to speak on what Islam has done for you.'* Well, 'Islam' had done a lot for me, so I just began to speak about this Great Teaching of the Honorable Elijah Muhammad, and the Great Word that I heard from Brother Malcolm; and the mosque, or temple, erupted with applause. And the next thing I knew, Brother

Malcolm put me in the Ministry Class, and my journey in The Ministry began.

But I was not in the mosque 30 days when a 'decree' had come down from the Honorable Elijah Muhammad: I was working in Greenwich Village in New York in a place called *The Village Bon*, so I wasn't at the lecture that day; so as soon as I got a break, I came up to the little Muslim restaurant, 'The Temple No. 7 Luncheonette,' to have bowl of that wonderful bean soup. And as I was sitting there, indulging in that beautiful bean soup with whole wheat bread, a brother came over to me and said, *'Man! You missed it today! Malcolm read a letter from the Honorable Elijah Muhammad, and in that letter he said all that are in 'show business,' all that are in 'music': They would have to get out of music, or get out of the temple.'*

I don't remember whether I finished my bowl of soup. I got up and walked out of the restaurant to think. ... I think I may have walked 30 paces, and I said: 'I can live without music, but I cannot live without The Truth.' And Brother Captain Yusef Shah ran up to me, wondering whether I had been 'ill-affected' by that command from Elijah Muhammad, and I told him I had made up my mind.

***

'Now, why are you saying this Farrakhan?' Well, I wanted to give you some 'background' on 'The Time and What Must Be Done.'

You know, in that letter that the Honorable Elijah Muhammad wrote, he gave '30 days to get out of show business.' And on *the last day* of the 30 days, I had an engagement at the *Nevele Country Club* in upstate New York; and I said, 'Well, I'm going get it all out of my system.' I went up in that country club and I sang ballads, I sang calypsos; I danced, I told jokes; I played jazz violin and I played classical violin. And I was finished. After I got it all out, I went down in my dressing room, and a man by the name of 'Purcell' came in my dressing room, who said: 'You are extremely talented. Do you have a manager?' I said, 'No sir.' He told me: 'I manage Pearl Bailey and Billy Daniels'—two of the greatest performers of their day; and he said: 'If you will let me manage your career, I will start you off $500 a week, and you will be playing in all of the supper clubs that take Billy Daniels and Pearl Bailey.' You say, *'Farrakhan, come on, now! I thought you were teaching 'Islam'?'* I am. Here is how: That man offered me more money, three or four times what I was making. At that time, in *1954* and *1955,* $150 a week was 'big money,' but to offer me *$500* playing in supper clubs across the country? That was a great offer! But I didn't tell him I wasn't going take it; I just said, 'Yes...' And he said, 'Well, when you come in the city, if you meet me tomorrow I'll have our lawyer there, and we'll sign a contract.'

I smiled and took the address of where we would meet, and I went back to my little apartment in Jamaica, Queens (New York). And that night I laid down in my bed, and Allah (God) gave me a Vision of 'Two Doors': One of doors had a sign over it saying **'SUCCESS'**—and I could look in that Door, and I saw a mound of *diamonds and gold.*

And right next to it was another door that had a 'Black Veil' coming from the top of the door to the bottom; and over that Door was **'ISLAM.'**
And I was told to *'Choose,'* and I chose The Door of 'ISLAM,' not knowing where that Door would lead me; but if I stayed in show business, I was guaranteed to have a mound of gold and diamonds. I chose 'The Unknown'—but what I *did* know was what I heard from Elijah Muhammad and Malcolm X of The Truth was what I was 'looking for' all my life! Mr. Purcell never saw me... I chose to 'give up the world' to *learn a Truth* that would free The Minds of Black People."

In the Honorable Minister Louis Farrakhan's historic Swan Song address, he shared with the world the numerous test he as a student was tried with by his teacher.

"I offered this man, Elijah Muhammad, my life. My songs were transformed from a nasty calypso or a stupid ballad into songs of the cause that brings about Resurrection. In 1957 at Elijah Muhammad's sixtieth birth anniversary, I sang for him, 'This Is The One.' It's on record. You can get it. Then in 1957, Brother Malcolm was writing in the Amsterdam News. His column was 'God's Angry Man' and Malcolm wrote 'A White Man's Heaven, Is A Black Man's Hell.'

But I sang the song, and it became an underground hit in the 1960s in the movement, 'A White Man's Heaven Is A Black Man's Hell.' I went into RCA Victor Studios in 1959 and my brother Thomas Jehad went into the studio with me. His job was to watch the engineer to make sure he didn't mess up my song.

One day Brother Malcolm asked me, 'Brother Louis where did you get that song?' See, we are little thieves at times. So Malcolm was testing me because he knew where I got it, but he wanted to know if I would say it. I said, 'Oh brother Minister, I read your column and I wrote the song.' It's exactly the truth.

If you want to know why I'm going up yonder, I earned my way. I earned my way.

I sang. I wrote plays. I preached. Every gift I had I offered it to my Teacher. Can anyone in here deny that? Hell no! You can't. You don't know anyone like me. I'm not boasting. I'm not bragging. God made me for Elijah.

So after that night at Dunbar High School in Chicago, the next morning, the Honorable Elijah Muhammad said, 'Brother, so you're back there again? Brother, your talent is great, but your greatest gift is in the spiritual,' he said. I didn't know that. He said, 'Would you give up all of that music for me?' I didn't even hesitate.

I said, 'Yes sir.' I said it so fast, he said it again, 'Would you give all this music up for *me*?' Because then he was going to teach me into the Spiritual Word of God that he alone knew that the Saviour taught him. I gave him my all. I'm not embarrassed. What did you get for it? How much money did you get? Nothing.

I came and sat at the table with my Teacher. He said, 'Brother Louis, a man came and offered $750,000 for the master of your song.' *The master of your song.* He knew who wrote it. He knew who it belonged to. He said, 'They offered $750,000.' This was back in 1956. Three quarters of a million dollars. So he asked me, 'Should I offer it to him?' I said, 'No sir, dear Apostle.' The Honorable Elijah Muhammad was trying to raise money to build a center. He needed money. Three quarters of a million dollars was on the table.

'Would you give me permission to offer it to them?' he asked. 'No sir, dear Apostle,' I said. Then he asked me, 'Why not?' He's locating me. The man asks you a question, once he locates you, he knows who the hell he is dealing with. He's not going to lay something on you and you're not fit. So, he has to try you.

Is three quarters of a million dollars a big enough trial? 'No. I don't care that we sell it because somebody will give you three quarters of a million dollars just to keep the song on the shelf. And Black people that I wrote the song for, put the truth of your teachings in that song, was so that they will be quickened to life.'

127

My brother Captain Sam, who became known as Abdul Rahman Muhammad, a great minister of the Honorable Elijah Muhammad. My brother was in Miami and he was selling Muhammad Speaks newspapers one day. Muhammad Ali, who was still Cassius Clay at the time, was across the street. And he shouted out, 'Why are we called Negroes? Why are we deaf, dumb and blind? Why is everybody making progress and we seem to be lagging so far behind.' And the Rock said, 'Hey man you hip, you hip to the Teachings.' How did he get hip to the Teachings? It was a sound made by Louis Farrakhan.

I offered the Honorable Elijah Muhammad my life. So, he begins spiritually teaching me. The Honorable Elijah Muhammad put Dr. Lonnie Shabazz on the national radio program representing him. He sent for me. *'Brother, how did you like Dr. Lonnie's teaching?'* I said, 'I love it dear Apostle, he was teaching your Teaching and I gained a lot from it.' See, he wanted to see if I was a kind of arrogant jackass that would say, 'I can speak better than he.
Why didn't you let me have the program?' See, Negroes can't hide. You can't hide. He took Dr. Lonnie Shabazz down and put up Bernard Cushmeer. After Bernard Cushmeer, now known as brother Jabril Muhammad, started teaching, the Messenger called me. *'What did you think of Brother Bernard?'* I said, 'It's wonderful. Dear Apostle, he's very knowledgeable. Anybody that knows, as you know, he's a very knowledgeable brother.'

I passed those two tests, then the Honorable Elijah Muhammad sent me a letter saying, 'Brother I was looking at you all the time.' Character. I don't care what you think you know. Your knowledge isn't worth a damn, if you don't have character that goes along with your knowledge. ... I'm saying all of that to say this. The Honorable Elijah Muhammad put me on the radio. The first four lectures he gave me a hint in the Teaching, he gave me a sentence or two and then I would take it from there. I sent the lecture out to him.

He passed it. The next week he passed it again. The next week he passed it again. The next week he passed it again. He said, 'Well, little brother you can keep going about six months or so.' And I used to say every week, 'The Honorable Elijah Muhammad, that great preacher of freedom, justice and equality to the Black man and woman of America, we're waiting his return to these microphones.' *Are you lying?* No. People lie once they get that lollipop and start sucking it.

For three years, I used to write out every single word. Then I would study each word, and if I could say it better by using another word, I would change that word for another one. Then I would rehearse, and I would broadcast.

After three years, the Honorable Elijah Muhammad said, 'Brother, you don't have to do that. Get a thought in your mind and a few scriptures and stand up and let God speak through you.' That's why you don't see me with notes. I don't give a damn about notes. I have studied so long and so hard, the notes are written on the inside.

Excuse me for saying damn. I have a little problem. But when you're dealing with us, if you don't curse sometimes, you'll be a killer. Don't you know we're a hard people to teach? So don't tell me, 'I'm a coward and I quit.' I got 67 years on you. ...

These are personal stories, but they're telling you something about why I'm going and why He's allowing me to come.

The Honorable Elijah Muhammad said, 'Brother, I want you to tell the people that I will be back next week.'

After five years, I done got the lollipop, sucked it until it's almost down, then you going to ask me to give you back the lollipop? That's a trial. I came back home and I went to writing, 'Harken to the Voice of God'—because that's who my Teacher is. I laid it out. He called back, 'Oh, brother, you may continue next week.' But what was he telling you, and what was he telling me, that I was so slow to accept? That I had become the Voice of God.

Now the biggest test that he gave me: Tony Brown, the great commentator, was inviting all the Black leaders to be on education channel. He invited Elijah Muhammad. Elijah Muhammad sent for me. He said, 'Brother, I'm not going to do that; I want you to do it.' I said, 'Me?' 'Yes. I'm going to show you how,' he said. And he starts teaching me how never to be afraid when you represent Divine Revelation.

So the Messenger called me for three weeks straight: 'Come out to Chicago. *I want to prepare you.*' A student being called by the teacher. He wants to prepare me; ooh I was so happy. He said, 'Now, brother, don't you be afraid of none of them because they have nothing to compare with what I've given to you. Stand up on it.' *Yes sir!* Finally the day arrived. Me and Brother Abdul Akbar Muhammad, and another brother, we're in downtown New York. I went out and bought a new suit. I was getting ready. I had laid out the Messenger's Teachings and I was fasting and studying and praying.

Finally the day had come. They were having a sound check in the studio, and I had to be there at two o'clock that day, so at one o'clock I called my Teacher. 'Dear Apostle, yes, I'm on my way to the studio.' *Notice the sound of my voice, you don't talk to the Boss raising your voice. You better show some submission here.*

I said, 'It's that day where that program is going to air.' 'What program?' asked the Honorable Elijah Muhammad. 'Oh, it's the program where all the Black leaders have been called,' I said. 'And who said you were one?' he asked. 'Oh no, dear Apostle,' I said. Then he hung up the phone. Let me tell you something, God taught the Honorable Elijah Muhammad how to try a person in such a way that whatever was hiding deep inside of them, they will not be able to hold it. If you try them as God taught him to try…

By the way, when he hung up on me while I was in New York waiting about the Tony Brown television show, I waited awhile and asked my friends, 'What should I do?' They said, 'Well, why don't you just call him back and ask him?' So, I called him back. He was having a diabetic coma, so he couldn't come to the phone. Well, it was time for the sound check. I wasn't there because I wasn't going anywhere until he gave me permission. Finally, he comes on the phone. I said, 'Dear Apostle.' In a sharp tone, he said, 'Well brother what do you want to do?' I said, 'I want to be with you, dear Apostle.' He said, 'Well come on then.'

I got on that plane and got to Chicago. He was going to do the broadcast all along. If I was the average Negro or devil ... 'he set me up like that. *Oh man he's terrible.'* (Smile.) Yes. But he had the soldiers out there. When I told him I was coming out, he had Supreme Captain Raymond Sharrieff sitting by me. He wanted to make sure that was where I really wanted to be. He didn't care if I messed up, he was going to fire me that night. See ,if you're with God, Brother Malcolm, what happened?

Fired him. Oh well. See, the great teacher. You can be great in your own eyes and great in the eyes of thousands of people, Elijah Muhammad doesn't care anything about that. He said, 'If I lost the whole of New York City, it wouldn't affect me.' That's my Teacher. One more mistake I made where he turned it into a trial in a lesson: When I got out there to Chicago, the broadcast came out. I was by his side, and I was bearing witness, 'Go ahead, dear Apostle teach!' You could always hear me. Wherever he was teaching, you would hear me bearing witness.

When I first arrived for the broadcast, I said, 'Dear Apostle, I'm happy to be here with you.' He said, 'I hope so.' He took his pen, he said, 'What is the name of this program?' 'It's called 'Is It Too Late," I said. *'Is It Too Late."* Well, it sure would have been too late for me if I didn't pass that test."

The Honorable Minister Louis Farrakhan passed that test. During an interview with Brother Jabril Muhammad in the historic book, "Closing the Gap," the Honorable Minister Louis Farrakhan shared the following words spoken to him by the Most Honorable Elijah Muhammad after the conclusion of the 'Is It Too Late' program.

"When it was over he said, 'Sharrieff' – 'Brother, you must be tired' – take him downtown, put him in the finest hotel downtown Brother Sharrieff and you come and see me in the morning for coffee.' But as I was going out the door, he said, 'Brother you passed a great test tonight.' I said, 'Yes, sir dear Apostle.' I went out the door. They took me to a fine hotel and put me up for the night. I went back to New York the next day. That was the trial. Three more and we can close this, although I could mention more."

The Honorable Minister Louis Farrakhan continues to show during The Swan Song address how he was tried by his teacher. He shared how the Most Honorable Elijah Muhammad tested his taking of correction in the presence of those who wanted to see him get in trouble after he visited Huey P. Newton.

"You remember Huey Newton of the Black Panther Party? I went to visit him, and I took some of the Believers. The minister from Los Angeles and the captain from Los Angeles and others, we all went to see Huey. When we got to Huey's apartment, his man came to the door. He said, 'Well, you can't come in unless you submit to a search.' Well, that wasn't no problem with me, we search everybody. Because my brother is valued in the sight of those who love him, I don't mind you searching me. I'm not carrying anything to hurt my brother. So, I submitted to the search. Oh, did my brothers eat my flesh.

The Messenger called me out to Chicago and he's whipping me, and he has my brothers right there watching the whopping. 'Here you are my National Representative, I put you in a million-dollar house and you go to this neuter gender and get down on your knees. I'm making you like the Pope.' Listen, the Pope doesn't accept questions like he is some common, ordinary man. The Pope comes out and gives you the encyclical. He gives you what he has to say and moves on. If you have a question you have to see the Pope. He said, 'I'm making you like the Pope.' Listen. 'And there you are bending your knees and bowing down to a neuter gender.'

Neuter means somebody who don't know who he is. He isn't this or that. And then after he beats me some more, the Honorable Elijah Muhammad said, 'Here you are second only to myself bowing down.' He whipped me some more. He said, 'You fell off the log brother. And when you're on a log and you fall off, you can't get up by yourself. You need help to get back up. Look at your leader, you're second only to me. They asked me to come the White House and I wrote them a letter and told them that, 'I live at 4847 Woodlawn Avenue. If you want to see me, you come to where I live. I'm not going to no White House." So, he's trying to tell me, don't bow down to this world. 'I'm making you greater than all of them.'

I took the whipping and came out stronger, came out better. I never had a negative thought about my teacher."

These are only a few of the trials the Honorable Minister Louis Farrakhan has shared. To learn about more, read pages 347-371 of the book Closing the Gap.

It's been reported that the Most Honorable Elijah Muhammad at the dinner table told his family how they did not love him the way the Minister does. He said that he tried everything he knew how to, to make the Minister hate him, and he could not do so.

Another reason the Honorable Minister Louis Farrakhan is the Number One Student of the Most Honorable Elijah Muhammad is because he is the first of the students of the Most Honorable Elijah Muhammad to go to Mecca and successfully defend The Cardinal Point of the Nation of Islam's Theology. In the lecture, "The Knowledge of God," the Minister discusses this experience.

"I shall never take that point from the back page of the newspaper, regardless to how many scholars don't like it. I visited Mecca and sat with the scholars. This (Point Number 12) was the main issue we wrangled over. When we finished, the scholars shut their mouths. They never had heard an exposition like that. What I gave to them, I am giving to you. Mecca could not defeat the argument I presented, though I am born in America and have never been taught in any Islamic school by scholars or scientists. I was taught by the unlearned one, the Honorable Elijah Muhammad. ... When I was in Mecca, the scholars, in their closing statement to me, said, 'Brother Farrakhan, when you get sick, you go to a doctor. You do not tell the doctor what is wrong with you, you ask the doctor to tell you what is wrong. When you are not knowledgeable, you come to the scholars and ask the scholars, that they may teach you.' And I responded, 'Who are the scholars? ... The doctors don't live any longer than their patients. I cannot trust the doctors' advice. It appears to me the scholars of religion are the ones who have ruined the world of religion. It seems to me, from my understanding of the Book—and you must bear with me, because I am just a child in this, but I am not a foolish child...'"

In the Swan Song, the Honorable Minister Louis Farrakhan went into more detail about what happened in Mecca.

"How could I go to Mecca? My son, Mustapha, can bear witness. The head of the Islamic League Dr. Abdullah Nassif heard me do a marriage ceremony in the National House. He was so impressed he wanted to introduce me to 150 imams in America, who were not thinking too well about the Nation of Islam. I said to Dr. Nassif, I would like for you to arrange for me to come to Mecca and meet the scholars about our Teachings. He said, I'll do it, and he sent for me.

Brother Leonard F. Muhammad is here. Brother Mustapha is here. Brother Jabril is watching. I want you to listen to this. My brothers were there. There was a Sheikh Zindani from Yemen. He was my first teacher that day. He came and from one hour and a half, he taught me. I took out a pad and I wrote down his questions, his responses and after he finished it was my turn. As Allah is my witness, I took everything that man said and with the Teachings of my Teacher I went to the root of what he was saying and taught him.

Listen now, the next day he came back and I came back the second day. He did the same thing, and I did the same thing. On the third day, they invited the great scholar Mohammad Kati, an Egyptian scholar. His brother is the founder of a great Islamic movement, The Muslim Brotherhood. He comes and now it's on Master Fard Muhammad and Elijah Muhammad. I wouldn't lie to you if they put a gun to my head. See, the truth is so powerful, but if you don't have the courage to stand up on what you believe, you'll be rolled over.
But that day, my son was in the back. He told me he was weeping because he saw his father with the scholars at Mecca. And when I talked about the Saviour and I talked about Elijah and defended them, one of the things I said, 'Now all Muslims that are here, you read the Qur'an. Name me one incident where Allah punished a people for their iniquity that happened again under Prophet Muhammad?' I'll wait.

I'm not going to have to wait long, because it never happened. I said, 'We're living in America. If Moses came back, he would run away if he saw Pharaoh, the Pharaoh I'm dealing with and Elijah Muhammad has been dealing with and the Black people that are torn to pieces by this devil.' I defended him. I defended us. After it was over, Sheik Zindani and I were walking together to perform Asr prayers. He said, 'Brother, well we'll just have to agree to disagree. I have not slept in three nights.'

See, a little Negro student of Elijah Muhammad coming to Mecca. You haven't seen me operating on the international scene at Al-Azhar University in Egypt. You don't know your brother. You are meeting him today probably for your first time. Excuse me for raising my voice. I just want you to see that I got one to raise and it ain't weak. **I just want you to know God is with me, and if you are with me, God and the Messenger are with you.**

Brother Leonard, my son and Jabril are witnesses, there was a tape of those three meetings. Brother Jabril had it and a fire took place and it was lost."

The Honorable Minister Louis Farrakhan has been offered millions of dollars by wealthy members of the Islamic world, along with promises to place him in a favorable place in history, if he would only stop teaching what he learned from the Most Honorable Elijah Muhammad. To these offers and more, the Honorable Minister Louis Farrakhan has refused. He speaks about this in the lecture titled, "The Majesty of Master Fard Muhammad's Love."

"When I decided with trepidation and some fear that I wanted to rebuild his work, I did not have any money or followers; I only had a desire. The scholars in the Middle East offered me millions of dollars to leave Fard Muhammad and Elijah Muhammad alone and preach Prophet Muhammad (PBUH).

One Arab said to me, 'If you do this, Farrakhan, we will back you; and when you pass on, we will tell the world that you were the Messiah.' They were trying to bribe me, thinking that I am doing this work to exalt myself. The enemy never wants to give a righteous man any righteous motivation.

Elijah Muhammad chose me to represent him because he knew that I loved you. I have always loved you, and I have given 50 years of my life to fight for our liberation. I have been evil spoken of, but you have never heard me speak evil of those who speak evil of me. I defend those who have been my enemies. I have power to kill my enemies; I have people around me that, if I just pointed my enemies out, they would be dead before sunset—but I would never misuse the love that I see that people have for me. I suffer what the people say. I suffer what the scribes write—knowing that, in the end, I will be the winner."

There are many who like to say that the Minister has deviated, that the Most Honorable Elijah Muhammad did not select him to sit in his seat in his absence.

They go on and on with their foolishness and their shielded disbelief in the Most Honorable Elijah Muhammad. When I engage them, I simply ask them, "How is it that a man that you call a hypocrite has and is doing more in the name of the man you say you are true followers of?" No, the Honorable Minister Louis Farrakhan is FAR from being a hypocrite, and his work, just like the rod of Aaron in the Bible, speaks for him.

Who was able to regain ownership of Mosque Maryam, the National House, the books of the Most Honorable Elijah Muhammad and the farmland? Was it the Minister, or his detractors? Who was able to call thousands of former and new followers back to the Nation of Islam? Was it the Minister, or was it his detractors? Who was it that took the name and legacy of the Most Honorable Elijah Muhammad from out of the trash can it was placed in, due to the mishandling of his domestic life? Was it the Minister, or his detractors? We all

know the answer to that! It was the
Honorable Minister Louis Farrakhan!!!

CHAPTER 10
The Accomplishments and Impact of the Most Honorable Elijah Muhammad

"By the mid-sixties, Mr. Muhammad's ever-growing Islamic movement extended itself to more than 60 cities and settlements abroad in Ghana, Mexico, the Caribbean, and Central America, among other places, according to the Muhammad Speaks newspaper, the religion's chief information apparatus."

...

"Under his leadership, the Nation of Islam began to show signs of progress with the establishment of farms, livestock and vegetable cultivation, rental housing units, private home construction and acquisitions, other real estate purchases, food processing centers, restaurants, bakeries, lamb packing and cold storage facilities, clothing factories, banking, business league formations, import and export businesses, aviation, health care, administrative offices, shipping on land, sea and air, plans for modern university and campus in Chicago in addition to men's and women's development and leadership training units."

— "The Honorable Elijah Muhammad; A Man Who Raised a Nation," The Final Call newspaper

"Elijah Muhammad has been able to do what generations of welfare workers and committees and resolutions and reports and housing projects and playgrounds have failed to do: to heal and redeem drunkards and junkies, to convert people who have come out of prison and to keep them out, to make men chaste and women virtuous, and to invest both the male and the female with a pride and a serenity that hang about them like an unfailing light. He has done all these things, which our Christian church has spectacularly failed to do."

— **James Baldwin, author of "The Fire Next Time"**

"Elijah Muhammad gave Blacks new confidence in their potential to become creative and self-sufficient people. In addition, he taught his followers the efficacy and rewards of hard work, fair play, and  abstinence. It has been shown beyond a shadow of a doubt that the Muslims who have followed his economic teachings and have in many cases moved substantially ahead in their economic pursuits. He also gave his people a success formula for home and family life. The rate of delinquency among Muslim children is extremely low. The rate of divorce is quite low. The stability of the Muslim home is an ideal for which the rest of America might strive."

— **Dr. C. Eric Lincoln, author of "Black Muslims in America"**

"We told our people, 'It's got to be done like the Muslims do it. It's got to be done person to person.' Of all the movements we know of, we have a lot of respect for you, because you have a lot of people doing things."

— **Cesar Chavez, leader of the Mexican American Farmworkers' Movement, referring to the constructive program of the Most Honorable Elijah Muhammad and its effect on his energetic followers**

"Approximately 30 percent of the United States' six to eight million Muslims are African American, making Islam the second most popular religion among African Americans. Although the vast majority of these African American Muslims are now Sunni Muslims, many (or perhaps their parents or grandparents) were introduced to Islam through the Nation of Islam, a movement that was exclusively Black, segregationist, and militant. Its leader for over forty years, Elijah Muhammad, was therefore arguably the most important person in the development of Islam in America, eclipsing other prominent figures such as Noble Drew Ali ... Malcolm X, Louis Farrakhan, and Warith Deen Mohammed (originally known as Wallace D. Muhammad). Despite his unrivaled prominence, Elijah Muhammad is rarely treated as a major figure in Islam.

— **Professor Herbert Berg, author of "Elijah Muhammad and Islam"**

"What the Negro needs first is $100 million," world famous composer Duke Ellington said last week in an exclusive interview with Muhammad Speaks. "And that  is the advantage your boss (referring to the Honorable Elijah Muhammad) has over the rest of the 20 million. He urges that we get some money together." "Without $100 million there is no voice. There are 20 million Negroes and we don't have $20 million." "MONEY TALKS in our society and economics is the big question throughout the world. Every race on this earth has some money but the American Negro..." This then is the solution to the "race problem" of the famous Duke, who is universally acclaimed as royalty in the realm of American music.

"We're here in honor of a man to be respected. In honor of a man who is very much deserved of the praises given to Him for His many deeds that most of us know very little about. I'm here, joining the others to give respect to a very beautiful man that I've seen do a lot with my brothers, people who I lived with; as a matter of fact—people that I am. He has most definitely been a positive influence ... I've got to respect this man for His works."

— Curtis Mayfield, legendary song writer and entertainer, during the occasion of Elijah Muhammad's Appreciation Banquet in 1974

"DEAR MR. MUHAMMAD,
An engagement of long standing in Madison, Wisconsin prevents my accepting your invitation to attend your testimonial dinner on March 29th. I do, however, want to extend my personal best wishes to you and my congratulations on your almost half a century of productive leadership.

— Letter from Vernon E. Jordan Jr., director of the National Urban League, in 1974

"These Black Muslim women looked at the Nation, and saw love and courage. To them the Honorable Elijah Muhammad was a man who loved his people so much that he designed an institution in which the primacy of women was integral, and every man in the organization was obligated to put himself on the line for them. Black Muslim women saw this as a measure of love and respect for them."

— Cynthia S'thembile West, scholar and author of "Nation Builders: Female Activism in the Nation of Islam 1960-1970"

"I, as many of you, sat at the feet of the Honorable Elijah Muhammad and shared and was taught. The Messenger made the message very clear. He turned alienation into emancipation. He concentrated on taking the slums out of the people and then the people out of the slums. He took dope out of veins and put hope in our brains. He was the father of Black consciousness. During our 'colored' and 'Negro' days he was Black. His leadership exceeded far beyond the membership of the Black Muslims. For more than three decades, the Honorable Elijah Muhammad has been the spiritual leader of the Black Muslims and a progressive force for Black identity and consciousness, self-determination and economic development."

— Rev. Jesse Jackson, civil rights leader and founder of the Rainbow PUSH Coalition

"Without question, he [Hon. Elijah Muhammad] aided many young Black Americans to gain dignity and hope and a will to survive. I have a great deal of admiration for the  sense of discipline he provided for many young Black men and women."

— John Lewis, U.S. Congressman, former head of the Student Non-Violent Coordinating Committee

"Mr. Muhammad's life is one of peace, harmony and great integrity. He made the Nation of Islam a pillar of strength in Black communities throughout the country."

— Ralph Metcalf, Former U. S. Representative 1st District, Illinois

"I tell people again and again and again that I know what I know not because of anything U.C. Berkeley (University of California-Berkeley) taught me, but because I learned what I learned in the Nation of Islam. I learned it from the sisters who learned it, basically, from Elijah Muhammad—and it worked! It changed a people who just like my Indian people, had a terrible diet. Still a lot of work needs to be done in the African-American community, but Elijah Muhammad was successful in alerting, millions probably, of African American people about pork and leading a healthier life."

— Diane Williams, MPH, Native American social worker

"The Hereafter means Freedom, Justice and Equality and I never knew anything about that until I started following the Messenger. When we first accepted Islam in Jersey City, N.J., the rest of the band was against it. They even tried everything to stop us from coming in. But now Islam is attracting them."

— Ronald 6X Bell, founding member of legendary and Grammy Award-winning band Kool & The Gang

"Once I heard the teachings of the Honorable Elijah Muhammad; that really touched me. It was something I could relate to and made me do better. Once you have heard the teachings (of the Nation of Islam) and know the knowledge, there is no turning back."

— Larry Johnson, former NBA All-Star

Although the Most Honorable Elijah Muhammad created the Three-Year Economic Plan (also known as the National Savings Plan) in 1964 with the express purpose of assisting Blacks in achieving financial independence, the Nation of Islam has always promoted economic self-reliance. He pushed Black people to make sacrifices for three years, spending only what they required and within their means to save money. He hoped that all Black Americans would abide by these rules in addition to advocating this program for Nation of Islam members.

For Nation of Islam members, however, the savings would be transmitted to the Nation of Islam headquarters in Chicago, where they would be used for group economic development projects, including the purchase of arable land for the cultivation of vegetables and the raising of livestock. The idea included encouraging Nation of Islam members to buy commercial real estate and forests.

With the timber, low-income Black people could construct homes. A clay-containing piece of land might be utilized to produce bricks, which could then be used to construct brick homes that could be sold to the poor at a reasonable price.

Nation of Islam members who could afford to committed one-tenth to one-third of their income to economic development as part of the Three-Year Economic Plan. Members had to either start their own businesses or buy Muhammad Speaks, the Nation of Islam 's official periodical, in order to support NOI-owned companies.

The Nation of Islam grew and consolidated Black money through its Three-Year Economic Plan to create organization-owned and member-owned firms by the early 1960s, when its membership had reached a peak of 70,000. These companies thereby supported the Nation of Islam's objective of establishing an independent, self-sufficient, and Black-controlled economy. The Nation of Islam established fifteen enterprises, including a clothes factory, Your Supermarket, Shabazz Grocery, Chicago Lamb Packers, Shabazz Bakery, Good Foods, Shabazz Restaurant, and Salaam Restaurant. By 1970, Nation of Islam enterprises were supplying both Muslims and non-Muslims with food, prepared meals, clothing, and dry cleaning.

Midway through the 1960s, the Nation of Islam built and acquired farms in Michigan, Alabama, and Georgia that provided meat and produce to urban supermarkets. Meat and food from these Nation of Islam farms were transported to Nation of Islam stores by a fleet of Nation of Islam vehicles and, at one stage, an airplane. This fulfilled a long-standing goal of Black nationalist organizations by establishing the first Black-owned national food manufacturing and distribution network.

Inner city people might work as managers, clerks, secretaries, bakers, cooks, butchers, waiters, accountants, mathematicians, technologists, plumbers, and carpenters, among many other positions given by Nation of Islam firms. Both Muslims and non-Muslims worked for Nation of Islam-owned companies. For instance, the Nation of Islam ran a dry-cleaning business in Chicago at 608 East 63rd Street in 1958. Herbert Muhammad, one of Elijah Muhammad's sons, oversaw the plant, which directly employed five Nation of Islam members full-time. Even though the company had two Nation of Islam delivery trucks, non-Nation of Islam members were also hired and frequently used their own vehicles to help with the pickup and delivery of dry cleaning in exchange for a commission of 35% on goods gathered from and supplied to clients.

From 1960 to 1975, Muhammad Speaks served as the Nation of Islam 's official publication, but it was also one of the business ventures that brought in the greatest money. Because it was delivered by a nationwide network of male NOI members, the publication expanded quickly. In 1969, the Nation of Islam printed the publication in one of its buildings with an all-Black printing staff using printing equipment that could make 50,000 copies in an hour. Muhammad Speaks had 400,000 copies printed each week by the end of 1969. The newspaper became one of the biggest Black-owned periodicals in the country when its readership increased to a record 950,000 in a single week in 1974.

Women made significant contributions to the Economic Development Plan while serving in leadership positions as captains, lieutenants, and secretaries, despite the Nation of Islam's recommendation that they prioritize domestic labor as wives and mothers. They also held positions as instructors, administrators, and principals at the University of Islam, one of the Nation of

Islam's parochial schools. In addition, women contributed to and edited the Muhammad Speaks publication, and others took up managerial and retail roles in the movement's enterprises. The daughter of Muhammad, Sister Ethel Sharrieff, also took part in these business endeavors. Sharrieff oversaw the Nation of Islam clothing store for women in Chicago, which occasionally recruited non-Muslims and had three full-time Muslim employees. The apparel shop also attracted a lot of non-Muslim customers. Some Muslim workers claimed they were more prosperous and comfortable financially than other Black people from comparable socioeconomic situations. They credited Muhammad's Three-Year Economic Plan, which enabled them to conserve money by removing the temptation to buy alcohol, tobacco, pricey clothing, and cars, with their financial stability. By keeping their diet to one meal per day, whenever possible, in accordance with Nation of Islam principles, they also managed to save money on food.

In the late 1960s and early 1970s, the Nation of Islam's economic growth agenda reached its zenith. The Nation had a sizable network of clients and workers in 1975, with an estimated 250,000 active members globally, ensuring the success of many of its businesses. The Nation of Islam started acquiring sizable existing enterprises after receiving this additional funding. The Nation of Islam paid $1 million for a four-story, 60,000 square foot building on Chicago's South Side in 1968. It served as a location for the Muhammad Speaks newspaper's operations. The Nation of Islam also spent another $1 million on a Chicago restaurant-supermarket (Salaam Restaurant and Your Supermarket) and another $100,000 on a lamb slaughterhouse that supplied the restaurant-supermarket with meat.

The Nation of Islam acquired a controlling stake in the Guaranty Bank and Trust Company in January 1973. Under Nation of Islam supervision, this South Side Chicago bank grew to have over $10 million in assets and more than 500 employees by 1975. This "bank for the black man," as Elijah Muhammad referred to it as, was evidence of the Nation of Islam's long-standing capital collection strategies and showed that the Nation was among the wealthiest Black groups in the country.

With its deal with a Peruvian fishing distributor to provide one million pounds of whiting fish from that South American country, Nation of Islam Enterprises had acquired an international scope by 1974. Nation of Islam members promoted the fish as being three times cheaper than land-produced meat, simpler to digest, and unlike catfish, whiting was not a "bottom feeder"; while selling it door to door in Black neighborhoods to both Muslims and non-Muslims. In 1974, Atlanta minister Abdul Rahman Muhammad estimated that only the month of September saw the sale of

200,000 pounds of fish. The Nation of Islam's fish program was so successful that the popular R&B musical group recorded songs that appeared on their album honoring the program and the economic program of the Nation of Islam.

"'Whiting H & G,' 'Hereafter,' and 'Fruitman' (songs from the album Light of the World) are meant to reflect a message of unity and seriousness from the Honorable Elijah Muhammad."

— Robert 9X Bell, founding member of the legendary and Grammy Award-winning band Kool & The Gang

By 1975, there were over 11,000 people employed by the Nation of Islam's hundreds of businesses spread across the Nation. About $30 million in annual sales was thought to be generated by these companies. The NOI's net worth was $80 million in 1975. By then, the Nation of Islam established more than 75 temples across the country with the use of its riches, which was also used to improve the financial stability of its members.

Chapter 11
How Can They Love the Fruit and Hate the Tree?

I personally believe that those who say they love the students of the Most Honorable Elijah Muhammad, as mentioned in this book, do not love the Most Honorable Elijah Muhammad, and do not really love any of those students as much as they claim. Think about this. Why does the world love Mary, the Mother of Jesus? It's because she is the vessel that held in her womb the man that they believe is the Messiah. A true lover of Jesus, the Messiah, would naturally love and appreciate his mother. One would look crazy talking about how they love Jesus while at the same time trying to minimize or outright ignore the role his mother had in and on his life. That's how I feel about those who try to praise the students of the Most Honorable Elijah Muhammad and minimize his impact on them. Why do they do this? I cannot say I wholeheartedly know the reason why they do, but I do have some thoughts I would like to share.

One, I believe it's a continued tactic of the modern Counterintelligence Program (COINTELPRO). Remember, in an internal memo, the FBI said they wanted to prevent the rise of a Black Messiah. Well, the Most Honorable Elijah Muhammad comes in fulfillment of the scriptures regarding the Messiah, God's Anointed; the person selected by God and filled with the knowledge, wisdom and spirit of God.

Two, it's an effort to continue to keep the masses, both Black, White and others, from realizing that the Most Honorable Elijah Muhammad was selected, raised and taught by God. If anyone would spend any time reading or listening to the words of the Most Honorable Elijah Muhammad, he/she would not be able to do so, not understanding that he believed and declared he was taught by God. So, to keep that from being realized, efforts are made to make it appear that his students just became great on their own.

Third, envy and jealousy. The Most Honorable Elijah Muhammad is a man who only completed the third grade, and yet he produced giants who turned this world upside down; many who were not "educated," according to this world's criteria, yet, they whipped many of the so-called educated and accomplished so much with a people who had been written off.

This book is my effort to leave something for those who love the Most Honorable Elijah Muhammad, those who want to learn more about him, and to serve as a barrier to those who want to write him out of history. I pray that the contents of this books inspired, educated and changed the minds of many who read it.

I pray that those who read this book take the truths found in it and post them on social media and quote them in educational essays/research papers. I pray that they reference the information in this book in barbershop discussions and Clubhouse debates. I also pray that this book inspires others to do even more in-depth scholarly works on this subject matter. Doing all of this will help to make the job of those who want to write the Most Honorable Elijah Muhammad out of history even more impossible.

I think that we have done a good job showing the impact of this marvelous man. Therefore, I just want to close with words I quoted from the Honorable Minister Louis Farrakhan in chapter one as a warning to those who seek to put out the light of Allah's Messenger, not realizing that they are setting themselves up for a great punishment.

"And now, there is a conscious effort to write the Honorable Elijah Muhammad out of history. However, I am sure that, by the help of God, everyone who plans to write him out of history has already assigned to themselves that chastisement."
– **The Honorable Minister Louis Farrakhan**

Made in the USA
Columbia, SC
09 February 2025

53282692R00107